PRESERVES

by
Jean Paré

Dedication

For a lasting impression.

Cover Photo

Countertop Courtesy Of:
P.F. Manufacturing Ltd.

Glass Jar With
Wooden Spoon Courtesy Of:
Mugsie's Coffee House

Glassware Courtesy Of:
The Bay Housewares Dept.

Pickle Dish Courtesy Of:
Eaton's China Dept.

Pottery Courtesy Of:
Alynn's Gallery For Gifts

PRESERVES

First Printing April, 1994

I.S.B.N. 1-895455-30-8

Published and Distributed by
Company's Coming Publishing Limited
Box 8037, Station "F"
Edmonton, Alberta, Canada
T6H 4N9

**Published Simultaneously in
Canada and the United States of America**

Printed In Canada

Company's Coming Cookbooks by Jean Paré

COMPANY'S COMING SERIES
English

HARD COVER
- JEAN PARÉ'S FAVORITES
  - Volume One

SOFT COVER
- 150 DELICIOUS SQUARES
- CASSEROLES
- MUFFINS & MORE
- SALADS
- APPETIZERS
- DESSERTS
- SOUPS & SANDWICHES
- HOLIDAY ENTERTAINING
- COOKIES
- VEGETABLES
- MAIN COURSES
- PASTA
- CAKES
- BARBECUES
- DINNERS OF THE WORLD
- LUNCHES
- PIES
- LIGHT RECIPES
- MICROWAVE COOKING
- PRESERVES
- LIGHT CASSEROLES *(Sept. '94)*

PINT SIZE BOOKS
English

SOFT COVER
- FINGER FOOD
- PARTY PLANNING
- BUFFETS

JEAN PARÉ LIVRES DE CUISINE
French

SOFT COVER
- 150 DÉLICIEUX CARRÉS
- LES CASSEROLES
- MUFFINS ET PLUS
- LES DÎNERS
- LES BARBECUES
- LES TARTES
- DÉLICES DES FÊTES
- RECETTES LÉGÈRES
- LES SALADES
- LA CUISSON AU MICRO-ONDES
- LES PÂTES
- LES CONSERVES
- LES CASSEROLES LÉGÈRES *(sept '94)*

table of Contents

Jean Paré was born and raised during the Great Depression in Irma, a small rural town in eastern Alberta, Canada. She grew up understanding that the combination of family, friends and home cooking is the essence of a good life. Jean learned from her mother, Ruby Elford, to appreciate good cooking and was encouraged by her father, Edward Elford, who praised even her earliest attempts. When she left home she took with her many acquired family recipes, her love of cooking and her intriguing desire to read recipe books like novels!

While raising a family of four, Jean was always busy in her kitchen preparing delicious, tasty treats and savory meals for family and friends of all ages. Her reputation flourished as the mom who would happily feed the neighborhood.

In 1963, when her children had all reached school age, Jean volunteered to cater to the 50th anniversary of the Vermilion School of Agriculture, now Lakeland College. Working out of her home, Jean prepared a dinner for over 1000 people which launched a flourishing catering operation that continued for over eighteen years. During that time she was provided with countless opportunities to test new ideas with immediate feedback – resulting in empty plates and contented customers! Whether preparing cocktail sandwiches for a house party or serving a hot meal for 1500 people, Jean Paré earned a reputation for good food, courteous service and reasonable prices.

"Why don't you write a cookbook?" Time and again, as requests for her recipes mounted, Jean was asked that question. Jean's response was to team up with her son Grant Lovig in the fall of 1980 to form Company's Coming Publishing Limited. April 14, 1981, marked the debut of "150 DELICIOUS SQUARES", the first Company's Coming cookbook in what soon would become Canada's most popular cookbook series. Jean released a new title each year for the first six years. The pace quickened and by 1987 the company had begun publishing two titles each year.

Jean Paré's operation has grown from the early days of working out of a spare bedroom in her home to operating a large and fully equipped test kitchen in Vermilion, Alberta, near the home she and her husband Larry built. Full time staff has grown steadily to include marketing personnel located in major cities across Canada plus selected U.S. markets. Home Office is located in Edmonton, Alberta where distribution, accounting and administration functions are headquartered in the company's own recently constructed 20,000 square foot facility. Company's Coming cookbooks are now distributed throughout Canada and the United States plus numerous overseas markets. Translation of the series to the Spanish and French languages began in 1990. Pint Size Books followed in 1993, offering a smaller, less expensive format focusing on more specialized topics. The recipes continued in the familiar and trusted Company's Coming style.

Jean Paré's approach to cooking has always called for easy-to-follow recipes using mostly common, affordable ingredients. Her wonderful collection of time-honored recipes, many of which are family heirlooms, is a welcome addition to any kitchen. That's why we say: "taste the tradition".

Foreword

In my grandmother's day, preserving food was a necessity to economize and to ensure an abundant winter food supply. Most families with a traditional rural background have a history of preserving their harvest of fruits and vegetables. Over the years, as more commercially canned products became available, the tendency to preserve foods became less important. Today, we have come full circle. There is very strong renewed interest by many to preserve fresh garden produce, not only for enjoyment and fulfillment, but also for the confidence in knowing exactly what is in every jar – fresh food, prepared by you, without unnecessary additives or chemicals. My own family takes great enjoyment in the delicious foods which line my pantry shelves.

PRESERVES contains recipes for everything from snacks, such as fruit leather and jerky (great for skiing), to a variety of savory condiments, as well as all the traditional pickles, jams, jellies, sauces, syrups and more. There are even recipes for baby food! No need to be intimidated – these recipes are easy and do not require an overwhelming time commitment. All recipes call for small quantities of ingredients which can be easily increased if you wish.

If fresh fruits or vegetables are not in season when you want to make jam or jelly, you may substitute fresh frozen ones which do not have any water or sugar added. Most of the jam, jelly and marmalade recipes in this book contain no added pectin. A few recipes are frozen, a few are dried. When preserved food has cooled, store in a cool dark area.

Preserving foods gives one a rewarding feeling of accomplishment. Try Spiced Plums, a family favorite from my great-grandmother. Chow Chow Maritime, is a must from my grandmother's and my mother's kitchen. Mango Chutney is really different, no one will recognize the fruit. Lady Ross Pickles taste as good as they look. Chicken Sausage and Picante Salsa are real party specials. You will no doubt be making more the second time around. To get started, check the list on page 8 for basic equipment required.

So much enjoyment will surely come from making and serving these special extras to family and friends, or when presenting them as a gift from your kitchen – especially when you can say with pride... "I made it myself".

Jean Paré

Equipment

Blender And/Or Food Processor: Use either appliance to chop, slice or purée food.

Canner: A large deep kettle with a rack or false bottom that keeps jars off the bottom of the pan. A lid is included. Holds 7 pints or quarts.

Cone Shaped Food Mill: Use to separate pulp from purée. It will also hold a jelly bag for draining juices from fruit.

Food Grinder: Use to grind fruit rinds for marmalades, or vegetables for relishes so that they don't become too mushy.

Jar Tongs: To lift hot jars by their necks.

Jars: A half pint refers to a 1 cup (225 mL) jar. A pint refers to a 2 cup (450 mL) jar. A quart refers to a 4 cup (900 mL) jar. New metric jars, 500 mL and 1 L are now on the market.

Labels: Use to identify the contents and to date each jar.

Large Pot Or Preserving Pan: Aluminum or stainless steel pots are suitable to use and should be large enough to hold four times the volume to be cooked. Enamel pots are not recommended as they get very hot and cause food to scorch. The pan must be large enough to allow for the huge expansion when cooking jelly at a full rolling boil. It should also be wide enough to allow for rapid evaporation of liquid when boiling down jams, chutneys, etc.

Lids: The snap lids are the best for sealing jars as you know very soon whether or not each jar is sealed. Wipe rims clean. As the contents of the jar cool, a vacuum forms ensuring a good seal. To secure lids, follow instructions that come with the lids.

Scale: A small kitchen scale is a useful item. It should be able to weigh up to 5 or 6 pounds (2.5 to 3 kg) of food.

Spice Bag: A double layer cheesecloth bag can be used for whole spices. A solid cotton bag should be used if spice mixture contains seeds, so they won't go through the cloth.

Spoons: Use long-handled spoons for deep-pot stirring and slotted spoons for removing food from hot liquid.

Tongs: To lift lids from hot water.

Unbleached Cotton And Cheesecloth: To make jelly bags and spice bags.

Wide Mouth Metal Canning Funnel: A big help for filling jars. It fits inside the neck of the jar and keeps the jar rims clean.

Glossary

Air Bubbles: Use a dinner knife or spatula handle to slide down inside of jar to remove any trapped air bubbles.

Fruit: Since under-ripe fruit contains more pectin than ripe fruit, try to include some if possible when making jams, jellies and marmalades. Marmalade can take a week to set, jellies up to 24 hours.

Hot Water Bath: Half fill canner with hot water. Place jars in rack. Lower rack to bottom. Pour in enough boiling water (not directly onto jars) to cover tops with 2 inches (5 cm) of water. Cover. Bring to a boil. Start timing. If needed, add boiling water to keep up level. Only foods, such as fruits and tomatoes, with high acid content can be processed in a hot water bath rather than using a pressure canner.

Jelly Didn't Set: The easiest and quickest remedy is to melt jelly down until hot. Soften one ¼ oz. (7 g) envelope unflavored gelatin in ¼ cup (50 mL) water for 1 minute. Stir into hot jelly to dissolve. This will set about 3 cups (675 mL) jelly. Re-bottle and re-seal.

Open Kettle: Jams, jellies, salsas, chutneys, relishes and ketchup, are cooked in a large pot or preserving pan. The heavier the pot, the better. The boiling hot food is poured into hot sterilized jars and sealed immediately.

Pressure Canning: Follow directions that are with your pressure canner.

Rolling Boil: A boil that cannot be stirred down.

Standing Time: Pickles should be allowed to stand for a few weeks before using so flavors mingle.

Sterilizing: Use your dishwasher to run jars through regular cycle to sterilize. Fill jars while they are still hot. Another method is to place open jars upside down in 3 to 4 inches (7 to 10 cm) of boiling water in a large pot. Allow to boil for 10 minutes. Leave jars in water until you are ready to fill them.

It is very easy to make your own baby food. Using a blender or food processor is helpful for making a smooth purée. If not, food must be rubbed through a sieve. Sugar, salt, or other spices are not added. Each ice cube is equivalent to about a 2 tbsp. (30 mL) serving. After thawing, add a bit of water or whole milk, if needed, to make desired consistency. Steaming food in a stainless steel vegetable steamer in your saucepan will retain optimum nutrients. Vegetable steamers flair out to fit a medium to fairly large size saucepan.

BEEF STEW PURÉE

Meat and vegetables all in one, which means more cubes per meal.

Lean beef, diced	1 lb.	454 g
Water	1½ cups	375 mL
Sliced celery	½ cup	125 mL
Green beans, cut up	8	8
Sliced carrots	1 cup	250 mL
Potatoes, cubed	2 cups	500 mL
Whole milk, more or less	1½ cups	375 mL

Cook beef in water for 20 minutes.

Add next 4 ingredients. Bring to a boil. Cook, covered, until vegetables are tender. Purée in blender.

Add enough whole milk to make desired consistency. Transfer to ice cube tray. Freeze. To store, remove cubes to plastic bag or container. Return to freezer. Makes 36 to 38 cubes.

PORK STEW PURÉE: Use cooked pork instead of beef. Proceed as above.

BEEF PURÉE: Use cooked beef and water only. Proceed as above.

PORK PURÉE: Use cooked pork and water only. Proceed as above.

VEAL PURÉE: Use cooked veal and water only. Proceed as above.

CARROT PURÉE

A cheery colored vegetable. Flavorful.

Carrots, peeled, cut in large pieces	**1 lb.**	**454 g**
Cooking water, more or less	**¼ cup**	**50 mL**

If carrots are fresh from the garden, brush rather than peel. If cut too small, they become too watery. Place carrot in steamer over boiling water in saucepan. Cover. Cook for 10 to 20 minutes, depending on age of carrots, until tender.

Purée carrot in blender, adding enough cooking water to obtain desired consistency. Turn into ice cube tray. Freeze. To store, remove cubes to plastic bag or container. Return to freezer. Makes 14 cubes.

Pictured on page 35.

GREEN PEA PURÉE

This will have to do until your baby is able to do the picking and shelling.

Fresh shelled green peas	**4 cups**	**1 L**
Reserved cooking water, more or less	**¼ cup**	**50 mL**

Place peas in steamer over boiling water in saucepan. Cover. Cook for 10 to 15 minutes until tender.

Transfer peas to blender. Purée, adding enough cooking water to make desired consistency. Turn into ice cube tray. Freeze. Remove cubes and store in plastic bag or container. Return to freezer. Makes 14 cubes.

Pictured on page 35.

CHICKEN PURÉE

Especially for the little toothless people.

Chicken breasts, halved, skin removed	2	2
Chopped celery	¼ cup	50 mL
Chopped carrot	¼ cup	50 mL
Water	1½ cups	375 mL
Broth or whole milk, more or less	5 tbsp.	75 mL

Combine first 4 ingredients in large saucepan. Cook, covered, 20 to 30 minutes until chicken is tender. Remove bones. Cut up chicken. Purée about ½ chicken and ½ vegetables with ⅓ cup broth. Repeat. Mix both purées in bowl.

Add more broth or milk as needed to make desired consistency. Turn into ice cube tray. Freeze. To store, remove cubes to plastic bag or container. Return to freezer. Makes 14 cubes.

Pictured on page 35.

APPLE PURÉE

Won't be long before an apple will be eaten out of hand.

Ripe, sweet apples (such as McIntosh)	1 lb.	454 g
Water	½ cup	125 mL

Remove stem and blossom ends from apples. Quarter apples, then cut smaller, leaving skin and core intact. Apples will be sweeter cooked this way. Place in saucepan. Add water. Cover. Bring to a boil. Cook slowly, for 15 to 20 minutes until tender. Press apples through food mill. Place in bowl. Stir in as much reserved juice as required to make desired consistency. Apples may be cored before cooking to put through blender. If your blender won't purée apple peel, apples may be thinly peeled before cooking. Turn purée into ice cube tray. Freeze. Remove cubes and store in plastic bag or container. Return to freezer. Makes 14 cubes.

Pictured on page 35.

BEET PURÉE

Some babies manage to get this on their cheeks where rouge usually belongs.

Beets, with at least 1 inch (2.5 cm) tops intact	1¼ lbs.	570 g
Water	3 cups	750 mL
Water, more or less	¼ cup	60 mL

Combine beets and first amount of water in saucepan. Cover. Bring to a boil. Simmer until tender. Use beets of the same size to cook evenly. Drain. Holding each beet under cold water, slip off skin. Discard tops.

Cut up beets and put in blender. Purée, adding enough water to make desired consistency. Turn into ice cube tray. Freeze. Remove cubes and store in plastic bag or container. Return to freezer. Makes 16 cubes.

GREEN BEAN PURÉE

A good green vegetable for baby to enjoy.

Young green beans	1 lb.	454 g
Cooking water, more or less	¼ cup	60 mL

Snap off ends from beans. Cut into 3 or 4 pieces each. Place in steamer over boiling water. Cover. Steam for 10 to 15 minutes until tender. Purée in blender, adding enough water to make desired consistency. Turn into ice cube tray. Freeze. Remove cubes and store in plastic bag or container. Return to freezer. Makes 14 cubes.

Paré Pointer

They gave their hens hot water hoping they would lay hard-boiled eggs.

PEACH PURÉE

Tasty, even to an adult.

Peaches, peeled and sliced, about 1½ lbs. (700 g)	**2 cups**	**500 mL**
Cooking juice, and water if needed	**⅓ cup**	**75 mL**

Dip peaches in boiling water for 1 minute. Cool in cold water. Peel. Slice, removing pits. Combine peaches and water in saucepan. Cover. Bring to a boil. Simmer for 15 to 20 minutes until soft. Purée in blender, adding enough juice and water to make desired consistency. Turn into ice cube tray. Freeze. To store, turn cubes into plastic bag or container. Return to freezer. Makes 14 cubes.

APRICOT PURÉE: Cook 1 pound (454 g) apricots and ¼ cup (60 mL) water. Do not peel. Cook 10 to 15 minutes. Proceed as above. Makes 16 cubes.

NECTARINE PURÉE: Cook 2 cups (500 mL) nectarines instead of peaches. It is not necessary to peel them. Proceed as above. Makes 14 cubes.

PEAR PURÉE: Cook 1½ pounds (680 g) pears, peeled, cored, cut and ⅓ cup (75 mL) water. Cook 20 to 30 minutes. Proceed as above. Makes 18 cubes.

PRUNE PURÉE: Rinse 10 oz. (280g) pitted prunes with hot water. Cook, covered, with 1 cup (250 mL) water for 45 minutes until soft. Purée prunes and juice in blender. Proceed as above. Makes 14 cubes of delicious sweet fruit.

STRAWBERRY BUTTER

Try this small recipe first then double it next time.

Fresh strawberries, whole	**3 cups**	**675 mL**
Lemon juice, fresh or bottled	**2 tbsp.**	**30 mL**
Granulated sugar	**2 cups**	**450 mL**

Grind or mash strawberries. Measure 2 cups (500 mL) and combine with next 2 ingredients in saucepan. Heat and stir on medium-high until sugar dissolves. Bring to a boil. Boil about 35 minutes until a spoonful cooled to room temperature on a chilled saucer remains smooth with no watery sign. Fill hot sterilized jars to within ¼ inch (6 mm) of top. Seal. Makes 1 half pint and 1 small jar.

Pictured on page 89.

PEACH BUTTER

Good flavored spread for breads of all kinds.

Peeled, pitted, ground peaches, about 3¼ lbs. (1.5 kg)	5 cups	1.13 L
Granulated sugar	1¾ cups	400 mL
Lemon juice, fresh or bottled	1 tbsp.	15 mL
Almond flavoring	¼ tsp.	1 mL

Place peaches in boiling water 2 at a time for about ½ to 1 minute. Peel. Remove pits. Grind or mash peaches. Combine pulp with sugar, lemon juice and flavoring in large saucepan. Bring to a boil on medium heat, stirring often. Boil, stirring often, for about 1 hour 15 minutes until thickened. A spoonful cooled on chilled saucer should remain smooth with no watery sign. Fill hot sterilized jars to within ¼ inch (6 mm) of top. Seal. Makes 2 half pints and 1 small jar.

APRICOT BUTTER: Use apricots instead of peaches. No peeling required.

PLUM BUTTER

This can be thickened in the oven or on top of the burner. A dark butter. A delicious spread.

Prune plums, halved, pitted	2½ lbs.	1.15 kg
Granulated sugar	2¼ cups	500 mL
Lemon juice, fresh or bottled	1 tbsp.	15 mL
Ground cinnamon	¼ tsp.	1 mL

Grind plums or run through food processor. Turn into 9 x 13 inch pan.

Add remaining ingredients. Stir. Cook in 325°F (160°C) oven, stirring every 30 minutes until thick. This will take about 2½ hours. Pulp may also be cooked in large saucepan, stirring occasionally at first, then more often as it thickens. A teaspoonful cooled on a very cold saucer should remain smooth with no watery sign. Pour into hot sterilized jars to within ¼ inch (6 mm) of top. Seal. Makes 2 half pints and 1 small jar.

APPLE BUTTER

One of the most used spreads. Great on muffins and loaves. Also good on a pork sandwich.

Tart apples, quartered	4 lbs.	1.81 kg
Granulated sugar	2 cups	450 mL
Lemon juice, fresh or bottled	3 tbsp.	50 mL
Cinnamon	1 tsp.	5 mL

Remove stems and blossom ends from apples before cutting into quarters. Place in large pot including seeds, core and peeling. Add sugar, lemon juice and cinnamon. Stir. Let stand until apples release some juice. Cover. Heat slowly. Bring to a boil. Cook gently, uncovered, stirring often, until apples are tender. Press through food mill. Turn pulp into small enamel roaster. Bake, uncovered, in 325°F (160°C) oven stirring every 30 minutes, until thick about 2 to 2½ hours. To test for doneness, cool a teaspoonful on chilled saucer. It should stay smooth. This may also be cooked in large pot on top of stove, stirring often. Pour into hot sterilized jars to within ¼ inch (6 mm) of top. Seal. Makes 4 half pints.

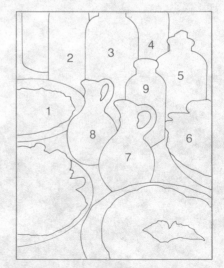

China Courtesy Of:
The Bay China Dept.

Glassware Courtesy Of:
IKEA Canada

Tablecloth Courtesy Of:
Reed's China And Gift Shop

BANANA BUTTER

A lovely flavored spread for scones, toast, or pound cake.

Mashed banana	1 cup	250 mL
Canned crushed pineapple with juice	1 cup	250 mL
Lemon juice, fresh or bottled	2 tsp.	10 mL
Chopped maraschino cherries	2 tbsp.	30 mL
Granulated sugar	3½ cups	875 mL
Liquid pectin	3 oz.	85 mL

Measure first 5 ingredients into large saucepan. Heat and stir constantly as you bring to a rolling boil. Boil 1 minute. Remove from heat.

Stir in pectin. Stir and skim for 5 minutes so fruit won't float. Pour into hot sterilized jars to within ¼ inch (6 mm) of top. Seal. Makes 4 half pints.

Pictured on page 143.

LEMON CURD

So smooth and tangy. Ready to fill baked tart shells any time. Once opened, store in refrigerator or spoon out quantity needed and return to freezer. Also called Lemon Cheese.

Large eggs	6	6
Grated rind of lemon	1	1
Juice of lemons	6	6
Granulated sugar	1¼ cups	275 mL
Butter or margarine	6 tbsp.	100 mL

Beat eggs in top of stainless steel double boiler. An aluminum pan may darken lemon color.

Mix in remaining ingredients. Cook over boiling water 15 to 20 minutes until smooth and thickened. Stir continually while mixture cooks. Mixture should pile softly when done. Cool. Fill containers leaving 1 inch (2.5 cm) headroom. Freeze. Keeps in refrigerator for 4 weeks after opening. Makes 3 cups (675 mL).

Pictured on page 143.

APRICOT CURD

A super filling for tarts. Very tasty. Also called Apricot Cheese.

Lemon juice, fresh or bottled	1 tbsp.	15 mL
Apricots, pitted and cut up	1 lb.	454 g
Large eggs, beaten	6	6
Granulated sugar	1¼ cups	275 mL

Place lemon juice in food processor. Add apricots. Process until fairly smooth.

Beat eggs in top of double boiler until frothy. Add sugar and contents of blender. Cook and stir continually over gently boiling water until sugar dissolves and mixture thickens and mounds softly. This takes about 15 to 20 minutes. Cool. Fill containers leaving 1 inch (2.5 cm) headroom. Freeze. Seal. Makes 4 half pints.

Pictured on page 71.

BANANA CHUTNEY

Contains dates and pineapple. A good condiment for any meat.

Medium onions, chopped	3	3
Medium bananas, diced	7	7
Chopped dates	2¼ cups	550 mL
Canned crushed pineapple with juice	14 oz.	398 mL
Raisins	1½ cups	375 mL
Crystallized ginger, chopped	4 oz.	113 g
Table salt	1 tsp.	5 mL
Curry powder	1 tsp.	5 mL
Mixed pickling spice, tied in double layer of cheesecloth	1½ tsp.	7 mL
White vinegar	1½ cups	375 mL
Granulated sugar	½ cup	125 mL

Place all ingredients in large pot. Heat on medium and bring to a boil, stirring frequently until sugar dissolves. Simmer, uncovered, for about 20 minutes until desired thickness is reached. Stir more often as it gets thicker. Discard spice bag. Fill hot sterilized jars to within ¼ inch (6 mm) of top. Seal. Makes 4 pints.

Pictured on page 125.

An ever ready appetizer to serve with crackers.

Cauliflower florets	2 cups	500 mL
Small white pearl onions, peeled and coarsely chopped	2 cups	500 mL
Green pepper, seeded and chopped	1	1
Red pepper, seeded and chopped	1	1
Sliced celery	1 cup	250 mL
Grated carrot	1 cup	250 mL
Ripe olives, pitted and coarsely chopped	1 cup	250 mL
Broken or cut green pimiento stuffed olives	1 cup	250 mL
Table salt	1 tsp.	5 mL
Pepper	$\frac{1}{8}$ tsp.	0.5 mL
Mixed pickling spice, tied in double layer of cheesecloth	2 tbsp.	30 mL
Canned tomato paste	$5\frac{1}{2}$ oz.	156 mL
White vinegar	1 cup	250 mL
Cooking oil	$\frac{1}{2}$ cup	125 mL
Water	$\frac{1}{4}$ cup	60 mL
Canned sliced mushrooms, drained	10 oz.	284 mL
Canned cut green beans or fresh, cooked	1 cup	250 mL
Canned flaked tuna, drained	7 oz.	198 g

Place first 11 ingredients in large pot.

In small bowl mix tomato paste, vinegar, cooking oil and water. Pour over vegetables in pot. Heat on medium, stirring often, until it comes to a boil. Boil gently for 45 minutes, stirring frequently to prevent scorching. Add a bit more water if needed to keep from burning.

Add mushrooms, green beans and tuna. Mix. Return to a boil for 1 minute. Discard spice bag. Put into freezer containers leaving 1 inch (2.5 cm) head space. Seal tightly and freeze. Makes 4 half pints.

Pictured on page 53 and cover.

APPLE CHUTNEY

Good with pork, goose or duck. Also good with any cold meat.

Tart apples, peeled, cored and diced	2¼ lbs.	1 kg
Medium onions, finely chopped	2	2
Coarsely chopped raisins	2½ cups	625 mL
Brown sugar, packed	3 cups	750 mL
Mustard seed	4 tbsp.	60 mL
Ground ginger	2 tsp.	10 mL
Table salt	1½ tsp.	7 mL
Cayenne pepper	¼ tsp.	1 mL
Cider vinegar	3 cups	750 mL

Combine all ingredients in large heavy saucepan. Stir over medium heat until sugar dissolves. Bring to a boil, stirring frequently. Boil gently, uncovered, for about 35 minutes until thick. Stir more often towards end of cooking time to prevent scorching. Pour into hot sterilized jars to within ¼ inch (6 mm) of top. Seal. Makes 3½ pints.

Pictured on page 125.

PINEAPPLE CHUTNEY

Chunky and brightly colored. Serve with ham or over cream cheese with crackers.

Peeled and chopped fresh pineapple or canned crushed pineapple with juice	4 cups	1 L
Cider vinegar	1 cup	250 mL
Brown sugar, packed	1 cup	250 mL
Golden raisins	1 cup	250 mL
Green pepper, seeded and minced	½	½
Toasted slivered almonds	¼ cup	60 mL
Garlic clove, minced	1	1
Ground ginger	½ tsp.	2 mL
Table salt	½ tsp.	2 mL
Cayenne pepper	⅛ tsp.	0.5 mL

Mix all ingredients in large heavy saucepan. Stir over medium heat until sugar dissolves. Bring to a boil. Simmer, uncovered, for about 35 minutes until thickened. Stir frequently as it thickens to avoid scorching. Fill hot sterilized jars to within ¼ inch (6 mm) of top. Seal. Makes 3 half pints.

CRANBERRY CHUTNEY

A glistening deep raspberry color. Tart with a hint of curry. Serve with poultry, ham or curries. Also good with fish.

Cranberries	4 cups	1 L
Raisins	1 cup	250 mL
Chopped onion	½ cup	125 mL
Tart apple, peeled, cored and diced	1	1
Prepared orange juice	1 cup	250 mL
Cider vinegar	1 cup	250 mL
Orange marmalade	½ cup	125 mL
Granulated sugar	1½ cups	375 mL
Ground ginger	1½ tsp.	7 mL
Table salt	1 tsp.	5 mL
Curry powder	1 tsp.	5 mL

Stir all ingredients together in large saucepan. Heat and stir on medium-high until sugar is dissolved. Bring to a boil. Cook, uncovered, for 10 to 15 minutes until thickened, stirring occasionally. Fill hot sterilized jars to within ¼ inch (6 mm) of top. Seal. Makes 3 half pints.

TOMATO CHUTNEY

Spicy, fruity, good. Serve with a cheese sandwich or as an accompaniment to beef.

Ripe tomatoes, peeled and chopped	4 lbs.	2 kg
Tart apples, peeled and chopped	3 lbs.	1.5 kg
Chopped onion	2 cups	500 mL
Green pepper, seeded and chopped	1	1
Raisins	2 cups	500 mL
Brown sugar, packed	3 cups	750 mL
Table salt	1 tbsp.	15 mL
Ground ginger	1 tsp.	5 mL
Cider vinegar	3 cups	750 mL
Mixed pickling spice, tied in double layer of cheesecloth	3 tbsp.	50 mL

Put all ingredients into large pot. Bring to boil over medium heat, stirring often until sugar dissolves. Boil, uncovered, for about 45 minutes or until fruit is tender. Discard spice bag. Pour into hot sterilized jars to within ¼ inch (6 mm) of top. Seal. Makes 6 to 7 pints.

PEACH CHUTNEY

Burnt-orange in color, this has a slight ginger flavor. Good with pork, duck and even over cream cheese served with crackers.

Peeled and sliced peaches	8 cups	2 L
Cider vinegar	2 cups	500 mL
Granulated sugar	3 cups	750 mL
Medium onion, finely chopped	1	1
Raisins	1 cup	250 mL
Chopped candied ginger	1/4 cup	50 mL
Garlic clove, minced	1	1
Table salt	2 tsp.	10 mL
Ground ginger	1/2 tsp.	2 mL
Cayenne pepper (optional)	1/4 tsp.	1 mL

Measure all ingredients into large pot. Stir over medium heat until sugar dissolves. Bring to a boil, stirring frequently for 45 to 55 minutes, until thickened. Stir more often near end of cooking time so as not to scorch. Pour into hot sterilized jars to within 1/4 inch (6 mm) of top. Seal. Makes 3 1/2 pints.

PEAR CHUTNEY

Serve this fruit chutney with poultry and pork. Try this spooned over cream cheese. Serve with crackers for a different appetizer.

Peeled, cored and diced pears	8 cups	2 L
Finely chopped onion	1 cup	250 mL
Coarsely chopped raisins	2 cups	500 mL
Granulated sugar	3 cups	750 mL
Table salt	1 tsp.	5 mL
Celery seed	2 tsp.	10 mL
Cayenne pepper	1/4 tsp.	1 mL
Curry powder	1/4 tsp	1 mL
Paprika	1/4 tsp.	1 mL
White vinegar	3 cups	750 mL

Mix all ingredients in large pot. Stir over medium heat until sugar dissolves. Bring to a boil. Simmer about 1 hour 10 minutes until thick. Stir more often as it thickens. Fill hot sterilized jars to within 1/4 inch (6 mm) of top. Seal. Makes 5 half pints.

Pictured on page 125.

RED PEPPER CHUTNEY

A tasty go-with for any meat. Terrific with cheese.

Tart apples, peeled, cored and diced	2 lbs.	1 kg
Large red pepper, seeded and diced	1	1
Large onion, finely chopped	1	1
Coarsely chopped raisins	¾ cup	175 mL
Table salt	1½ tsp.	7 mL
Prepared mustard	2 tsp.	10 mL
Ground ginger	½ tsp.	2 mL
Cayenne pepper	⅛ tsp.	0.5 mL
Granulated sugar	1 cup	250 mL
White vinegar	1½ cups	375 mL

Combine all ingredients in heavy pot. Stir over medium heat until sugar dissolves. Bring to a boil. Simmer, uncovered, about 1 hour until thick. Stir more often as cooking time increases so it won't scorch. Fill hot sterilized jars to within ¼ inch (6 mm) of top. Seal. Makes 5 half pints.

Variation: Half green tomatoes and half apples may be used.

APRICOT CHUTNEY

Spicy tan color. Especially good with cheese, ham and curries. Try it in a sandwich.

Fresh apricots, chopped	2 lbs.	1 kg
Red onions, diced	2	2
Raisins	2 cups	500 mL
Brown sugar, packed	3 cups	750 mL
Cider vinegar	2½ cups	625 mL
Chili powder	1 tsp.	5 mL
Mustard seed	1 tsp.	5 mL
Table salt	1 tsp.	5 mL
Curry powder	¼ tsp.	1 mL
Turmeric	¼ tsp.	1 mL
Ground cinnamon	¼ tsp.	1 mL

Place all ingredients in large pot. Stir over medium heat until sugar dissolves. Bring to a boil, stirring often. Simmer, uncovered, for about 1 hour until thick. Stir more often as it thickens to prevent scorching. Pour into hot sterilized jars to within ¼ inch (6 mm) of top. Seal. Makes 3½ pints.

MANGO CHUTNEY

A great accompaniment for curries and lamb. Good with or without cayenne pepper.

Green mangoes, peeled and cut up	4 lbs.	2 kg
White vinegar	2 cups	500 mL
Raisins (golden is best)	1/2 cup	125 mL
Currants	1/2 cup	125 mL
Garlic clove, minced	1	1
Ground ginger	1 tsp.	5 mL
Coarse (pickling) salt	1 tsp.	5 mL
Cayenne pepper	1/4 tsp.	1 mL
Mustard powder	1/8 tsp.	0.5 mL
Granulated sugar	1 1/2 cups	375 mL

Combine first 9 ingredients in large pot. Bring to a boil over medium-high heat, stirring often. Simmer slowly, stirring occasionally, for 20 minutes until mango is soft and a bit mushy.

Stir in sugar. Cook 10 minutes more, stirring once in a while until sugar dissolves. Pour into hot sterilized jars to within 1/4 inch (6 mm) of top. Seal. Makes 5 half pints.

Pictured on cover.

SASSY SALSA

A bit of a nip. Easy to make hotter or cooler by adjusting the amount of crushed chilies.

Ripe tomatoes, peeled and chopped	4 1/2 lbs.	2 kg
Medium onions, chopped	3	3
White vinegar	1/4 cup	60 mL
Dried crushed chillies, (crushed red pepper)	1 tsp.	5 mL
Table salt	1 1/2 tsp.	7 mL
Pepper	1/4 tsp.	1 mL
Canned chopped green chilies	2 x 4 oz.	2 x 114 mL
Granulated sugar	1 tsp.	5 mL
Paprika	1 1/2 tsp.	7 mL

(continued on next page)

Combine all ingredients in large pot. Bring to a boil on medium-high heat, stirring often. Boil gently until thickened. This will take about 1½ hours. Pour into hot sterilized jars to within ¼ inch (6 mm) of top. Seal. This may also be frozen in whatever size container you wish. Makes 3 pints.

RHUBARB CHUTNEY

A good, mild spicy flavor. Excellent served with cold meat, as a sandwich spread or over cream cheese with crackers.

Sliced rhubarb	8 cups	2 L
White vinegar	2 cups	500 mL
Granulated sugar	2 cups	500 mL
Brown sugar, packed	2 cups	500 mL
Golden raisins	2 cups	500 mL
Finely chopped onion	2 cups	500 mL
Table salt	½ tsp.	2 mL
Ground ginger	½ tsp.	2 mL
Cayenne pepper	¼ tsp.	1 mL
Mustard seed	1 tbsp.	15 mL
Cinnamon stick, broken up	1	1
Whole cloves	1 tsp.	5 mL

Mix first 9 ingredients in large heavy pot.

Tie mustard seed, cinnamon stick and cloves in double layer of cheesecloth. Add to pot. Heat on medium, stirring often as it comes to a boil and sugar dissolves. Simmer, uncovered, for about 40 minutes until thickened, stirring occasionally. Discard spice bag. Pour into hot sterilized jars to within ¼ inch (6 mm) of top. Seal. Makes 3 pints.

Paré Pointer

Lemonade? That's when you help an old lemon across the street.

PICANTE SALSA

The heat in this chunky salsa is adjustable. Excellent.

Ripe tomatoes, scalded, peeled and chopped	4½ lbs.	2 kg
Mild green chilies, chopped	3	3
Large Spanish onion, chopped	1	1
Large green pepper, chopped	1	1
Medium red pepper, chopped	1	1
Canned whole jalapeño peppers, chopped	3-6	3-6
Tomato paste	5½ oz.	156 mL
White vinegar	¾ cup	175 mL
Brown sugar	¼ cup	50 mL
Coarse (pickling) salt	1 tbsp.	15 mL
Paprika	2 tsp.	10 mL
Garlic powder (or 2 cloves, minced)	½ tsp.	2 mL

Combine all ingredients in large pot. Bring to a boil, uncovered, over medium heat stirring occasionally. Boil gently for 60 minutes, stirring occasionally, until thickened to desired consistency. Close to the end of cooking, taste to see if you would like to add more jalapeño peppers. Add as many more as you like. Pour into hot sterilized jars to within ¼ inch (6 mm) of top. Seal. Serve with nachos that have melted cheese, sour cream and green onions on them. Also good with quesadillas and sour cream, or burgers. Makes 10 half pints or 5 pints.

Pictured on cover.

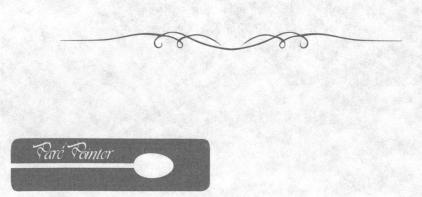

Paré Pointer

The shortened form for cannot is can't. The shortened form for doughnut is don't.

SIMPLE PICANTE SALSA

For a mild, chunky salsa, simply omit the crushed red chilies. For hot salsa, add more. Easy to double.

Canned tomatoes, chopped (see Note)	28 oz.	796 mL
Canned tomato sauce	7¹/₂ oz.	213 mL
Garlic clove, minced	1	1
Small green pepper, seeded and chopped	1	1
Small red pepper, seeded and chopped	1	1
Dried whole oregano	¹/₂ tsp.	2 mL
Coarse (pickling) salt	¹/₂ tsp.	2 mL
Dried crushed red chili peppers	¹/₂ tsp.	2 mL

Combine all ingredients in large saucepan. Bring to a boil over medium heat. Continue to boil gently for about 20 minutes, stirring occasionally until thickened. Cool. Pour into containers to within 1 inch (2.5 cm) of top. Freeze. Makes 3 half pints.

Pictured on page 53.

Note: If using fresh tomatoes, peel and cook 2¹/₃ pounds (1 kg).

LEMONADE CORDIAL

Just stir lemonade ice cubes with water to make a quick refreshing drink.

Granulated sugar	6 cups	1.35 L
Water	3 cups	675 mL
Tartaric acid (buy in drugstore)	5 tsp.	25 mL
Lemon juice, about 6 lemons	1 cup	250 mL
Water	3 cups	675 mL

Place sugar, first amount of water and tartaric acid in saucepan. Heat and stir until sugar dissolves. Remove from heat.

Stir in lemon juice and second amount of water. Fill ice cube trays, using 2 tbsp. (30 mL) per cube. Freeze. To store, remove cubes to plastic bag or container. To serve, use 3 parts water to 1 part cordial or 2 cubes to ³/₄ cup (175 mL) water. Stir briefly to combine. Makes 84 cubes.

Pictured on page 35.

TOMATO JUICE

You will want to increase the recipe if you have a good tomato supply.

Ripe, firm tomatoes, unpeeled, cut in small pieces	5 lbs.	2.27 kg
Table salt, for each pint of juice	½ tsp.	2 mL

Place tomato pieces in large pot. Bring to boil over medium heat, stirring occasionally. Simmer, with bubbles barely breaking surface, until tomatoes are soft. Put through sieve or food mill. Turn juice into pot. Heat again almost to boiling. Add salt to each jar. Pour juice into hot sterilized jars to within ¼ inch (6 mm) of top. Seal. Store in dark, cool area to keep color from being affected. Makes 3½ pints.

RASPBERRY CORDIAL

With a bottle of this in the refrigerator, a quick drink is always but a step away.

Raspberries	4 cups	1 L
White vinegar to cover		
Granulated sugar, equal to juice		

Fill quart jar with raspberries, shaking it as you fill. Add vinegar to cover raspberries. Cover. Let stand on counter for 2 days. Strain.

Measure juice and pour into saucepan. Add same quantity of sugar. Heat and stir to dissolve sugar. Boil rapidly for 10 minutes. Cool. To serve, mix 1 part cordial to 3 parts water. Store on shelf. Makes 2¼ cups (500 mL) cordial.

Pictured on page 71.

STRAWBERRY CORDIAL: Fill quart jar with cut up strawberries rather than raspberries. Makes 3 cups (675 mL) cordial.

NANKING CHERRY CORDIAL: Use same method as above except when you strain off juice, crush cherries with bottom of water glass to break skins, then strain cherries again. Makes 2¼ cups (500 mL) cordial.

Very special served over ice cream. Also good on cottage cheese, custard or vanilla pudding.

| Strawberries, hulled (see Note) | 1 lb. | 500 g |
| Granulated sugar | 2 cups | 500 mL |

White rum to cover fruit

Additional assorted fruit, apricots, peeled peaches, etc. (cherries shrivel)

This is a recipe of proportions. Begin with one of the first fruits of the season. Put equal proportions of fruit and sugar, 1 cup (250 mL) of each, into small crock or large jar. Stir lightly. Cover and let stand until strawberries release some juice.

Pour rum over top until it reaches ½ to ¾ inch (12 to 18 mm) above top of fruit. Stir to dissolve sugar. Place plate or bowl over top to keep fruit submerged. Cover loosely and store in cool place for 4 weeks.

Add the next fruit in season. Slice or cube as desired. Add 1 cup (250 mL) sugar to 1 cup (250 mL) fruit. Add more rum to reach above fruit again. Allow 1 week after adding last fruit before eating.

Note: Several fruits may be used at first following the same proportions of fruit and sugar. Cover fruit with rum. You can simply use a larger quantity of only 1 fruit if you desire. Keeps indefinitely as long as fruit is covered with rum. Makes whatever quantity you choose.

The easiest no-fuss way to can fruit.

Fruit of your choice

| Granulated sugar, per quart (see Note) | ¾ cup | 175 mL |
| Boiling water | | |

Pack jar half full with fruit. Pour sugar over top. Pack with more fruit leaving 1 inch (2.5 cm) headroom. Fill with boiling water to within ½ inch (12 mm) of top. Secure lid. Turn jar over a few times to start sugar dissolving. Process in hot water bath 20 minutes. Makes any quantity you like.

Note: Use 6 tbsp. (90 mL) granulated sugar per pint.

Variation: You may use ⅔ cup (150 mL) sugar per quart and ⅓ cup (75 mL) per pint as a bit less sweet variation.

PEACHES

Some of the most common favorite fruits are listed below.

Peaches, per quart	**1¼ lbs.**	**570 g**
SYRUP PROPORTION		
Granulated sugar	**1 cup**	**250 mL**
Water	**2 cups**	**500 mL**

Immerse peaches in boiling water for ½ to 1 minute. Run under cold water. Peel. Cut in half. Discard pits. Either slice or pack halves into hot sterilized jars to within 1 inch (2.5 cm) of top. Pack firmly without bruising fruit.

Syrup Proportion: First fill 1 jar of fruit with water. Drain and measure. Multiply the amount by the number of jars and you will know how much syrup to make. Measure sugar and water into saucepan. Heat on medium-high stirring occasionally until it boils. You will have about 2½ cups (625 mL) syrup. Pour over fruit to within ½ inch (12 mm) of top. Secure lids. Process in hot water bath for 25 minutes for quarts, 20 minutes for pints. Makes as many jars as your canner will hold.

APRICOTS/PRUNE PLUMS: Do not peel. Halve and pit. Pack into jars. Proceed as for Peaches. You will need about 1¼ pounds (570g) per quart.

CHERRIES: Remove stems. Pack into jars. Proceed as for Peaches. You will need about 1 pound (454 g) per quart.

CRABAPPLES: Leave stems attached. Remove blossom ends. Small crabapples will take about ¾ pound (340 g) per quart. Prick skin before packing. Proceed as for Peaches.

BLUEBERRIES/SASKATOONS: One quart takes about 1 pound (454 g) blueberries. Proceed as for Peaches but process quarts 15 minutes, pints 10 minutes.

PEARS: Stem, peel, quarter and core. One quart will need about 1½ pounds (680 g). Proceed as for Peaches.

STRAWBERRIES, RASPBERRIES, LOGANBERRIES: Pack berries into jars, pressing down rather firmly. One quart will take about 1 pound (454 g). Use 1 cup (250 mL) sugar to 1 cup (250 mL) water. Proceed as for Peaches, but process 20 minutes for quarts, 15 minutes for pints.

A favorite extra to serve hot or cold with the main course.

Peaches, peeled and sliced	3	3
Pears, peeled, cored and sliced	3	3
Apricots, pitted and sliced	9	9
Canned pineapple tidbits	19 oz.	540 mL
Raisins	1 cup	250 mL
Maraschino cherries, drained, halved or whole	1 cup	250 mL
Butter or margarine	½ cup	125 mL
All-purpose flour	4 tbsp.	60 mL
Curry powder	1 tbsp.	15 mL
Granulated sugar	1½ cups	375 mL
Water	2 cups	500 mL

Boiling water, if needed

Combine first 6 ingredients in large bowl. Toss to distribute evenly. Pack into 5 hot sterilized pint jars to within 1 inch (2.5 cm) of top.

Melt butter in saucepan. Mix in flour and curry powder. Add sugar. Stir in first amount of water over medium heat until it boils and thickens. Divide among jars, using dinner knife to move fruit around so liquid will go down evenly around fruit.

Fill with boiling water, if needed, to within ¼ inch (6 mm) of top. Secure lids. Process in hot water bath for 20 minutes. Makes 5 pints.

Pictured on page 125.

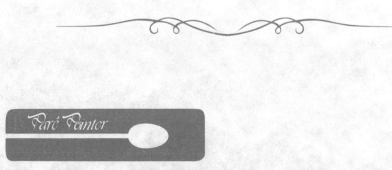

Paré Pointer

Little Jennie was asked in class to draw a horse and cart. She just drew the horse then let the horse draw the cart.

JELLY BAG: Lay a good size piece of unbleached cotton or double layer of cheesecloth in a large bowl. Pour fruit and juice on cloth. Gather top, tie, raise bag, suspend over bowl tying bag to cupboard door handle or place in food mill over bowl.

SEALING JARS: Wipe jar rims clean. Use lids that will seal or if not, melt paraffin wax, allowing about 1 tbsp. (15 mL) per jar. For a handy container, wash and dry a can from canned vegetables. Press in the top sides to form a pouring spout. Add wax. Melt over low heat being careful not to overheat. Pour a thin coating over hot jelly. For easy removal of wax, lay a short overhanging piece of string on top. Cover with a second thin layer of wax when first layer is almost set. To store cover jar with lid or plastic wrap.

TEST FOR JELLIES: Place about 1 tsp. (5 mL) jelly on chilled saucer. Chill. It should form a top skin, not run on saucer. A path drawn through with a spoon should remain intact. Remove pot from heat when testing to prevent overcooking. Another method is to use a candy thermometer. Temperature should be 8°F (4°C) higher than boiling water. Sea level would be 212°F (100°C) plus 8°F (4°C) which would equal 220°F (104°C). Cook, uncovered.

TEST FOR JAMS, CONSERVES AND MARMALADES: Similar to the test for jelly. If there isn't much pectin in fruit, the cold sample test should be thick enough to spread. Conserves will be a bit softer.

1. Barbecue Sauce page 136
2. Lemonade Cordial page 29
3. Sweet Dill Pickles page 93
4. Golden Relish page 119
5. Apple Purée page 12
6. Carrot Purée page 11
7. Green Pea Purée page 11
8. Chicken Purée page 12
9. Winter Chili Sauce page 133
10. Sweet Pickle Relish page 130
11. Ketchup page 139
12. Hamburger Patties page 111
13. Golden Mustard page 145
14. Strawberry Leather page 55

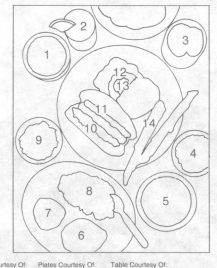

BEET JELLY WITH LEMON

An elusive flavor. You can imagine you are eating an exotic fruit.

Large beets, peeled and cut up	6	6
Water	5 cups	1.13 L
Reserved beet juice, plus water (if needed) to measure	3 cups	675 mL
Packaged lemon drink powder, without sugar (such as Kool Aid)	1 x ¼ oz	1 x 8 g
Pectin crystals	1 x 2 oz.	1 x 57 g
Granulated sugar	4 cups	900 mL
Table salt, just a pinch		

Cook beets in water until tender. Drain and reserve juice.

Combine reserved juice, drink powder and pectin in large pot. Stir and bring to a boil over medium-high heat. Boil 6 minutes without stirring.

Stir in sugar and salt. Return to a boil. Boil rapidly on high for 1 minute. Skim off foam. Pour into hot sterilized jars to within ¼ inch (6 mm) of top. Seal. Makes 4 half pints.

RASPBERRY JELLY

Clear and ruby red. Perfect toast-mate. Also a good custard topping.

Raspberries (about 5 pint baskets)	10 cups	2.25 L
Pectin crystals	1 x 2 oz.	1 x 57 g
Granulated sugar	5 cups	1.13 L

Place raspberries in large pot. Mash with potato masher. Heat just enough to warm a bit so juice runs better. Turn into jelly bag to drain. Pour 4 cups (900 mL) measured juice into large pot.

Stir in pectin crystals. Stir over medium-high heat until it boils.

Add sugar. Stir until it boils again. Bring to a full rolling boil. Boil 4 minutes. Remove from heat. Skim off foam. Pour into hot sterilized jars to within ¼ inch (6 mm) of top. Seal. Makes 6 half pints.

STRAWBERRY JAM SPOOF

Not a berry in it. The texture comes from the other fruit and the flavor from gelatin. Try it. It is so easy.

Rhubarb, cut in 1 inch (2.5 cm) lengths	8 cups	1.8 L
Granulated sugar	5 cups	1.1 L
Crushed pineapple with juice	1 cup	250 mL
Strawberry flavored gelatin (jelly powder)	2 × 3 oz.	2 × 85 g

Combine rhubarb and sugar in bowl. Cover. Let stand overnight on counter. Transfer rhubarb mixture to saucepan. Bring to a boil. Simmer, uncovered, for 15 minutes.

Add pineapple with juice and gelatin. Stir and boil for 1 minute. Skim off foam. Pour into hot sterilized jars to within ¼ inch (6 mm) of top. Seal. Makes about 8 half pints.

Pictured on page 89.

PEACH JAM SPOOF: Omit pineapple and juice. Use peach flavored gelatin instead of strawberry. An excellent flavor.

RASPBERRY JAM SPOOF: Use raspberry gelatin instead of strawberry. Use 6 cups (1.35 L) granulated sugar.

Pictured on cover.

Paré Pointer

The main reason ghosts are invisible is that they wear see-through clothes.

STRAWBERRY FREEZER JAM

Excellent flavor and color. Soft enough to top ice cream.

Sliced strawberries, buy about 3 pint baskets	4 cups	1 L
Granulated sugar	2 cups	500 mL
Granulated sugar	2 cups	500 mL
Lemon juice, fresh or bottled	2 tbsp.	30 mL

Place strawberries in large pot. Cover with first amount of sugar. Heat and stir on high until it comes to a full rolling boil. Boil hard for 3 minutes, stirring continually.

Add remaining sugar. Return to a boil, stirring continually. Boil hard for 3 more minutes while continuing to stir. Remove from heat.

Add lemon juice. Stir and skim off foam. Cool. Fill jars or plastic containers leaving at least 1 inch (2.5 cm) at top for expansion. Let stand on counter 24 hours to set. Freeze. Makes 4 half pints.

BLACK CURRANT JELLY

Clear, dark and delicious. Good for toast, topping for vanilla pudding or as a sauce for meatballs.

Black currants	5 cups	1.13 L
Water	3 cups	675 mL
Prepared juice, plus water if needed	4¼ cups	950 mL
Pectin crystals	1 × 2 oz.	1 × 56 g
Granulated sugar	4½ cups	1 L
Lemon juice, fresh or bottled	3 tbsp.	50 mL

Using bottom of jar, mash currants in large pot. Add water. Bring to a boil. Simmer for 10 minutes. Turn into jelly bag. Drain overnight.

Measure juice, adding water to make right quantity. Combine with pectin in large pot. Bring to a rolling boil, stirring continually.

Add sugar and lemon juice. Stir to dissolve sugar. Return to a rolling boil. Boil hard for 1 minute without stirring. Skim off foam. Pour into hot sterilized jars to within ¼ inch (6 mm) of top. Seal. Makes 6 half pints.

WINE JELLY

Tastes like your favorite wine. Makes a different gift.

Red wine, your favorite, not too sweet	4 cups	900 mL
Granulated sugar	6 cups	1.35 L
Liquid pectin	6 oz.	170 mL

Combine wine and sugar in large pot. Heat on high and stir occasionally as it comes to a rolling boil.

Add liquid pectin. Return to a rolling boil. Boil hard for 1 minute. Skim off foam. Pour into hot sterilized jars to within ¼ inch (6 mm) of top. Seal. Makes 8 half pints.

Pictured on page 89.

GOLDEN WINE JELLY: Use pale sherry in place of red wine.

PORT WINE JELLY: Use port in place of red wine. Makes a gorgeous ruby-red color.

PURPLE WINE JELLY: Use concord grape wine instead of red wine.

BEET-RASPBERRY JELLY

Easier than picking and cleaning raspberries. Good raspberry flavor. Gorgeous color.

Large beets, peeled and cut up (about 6)	4 lbs.	1.8 kg
Water	5 cups	1.13 L
Reserved beet juice, plus water (if needed) to measure	3 cups	675 mL
Lemon juice, fresh or bottled	3 tbsp.	50 mL
Pectin crystals	1 × 2 oz.	1 × 57 g
Granulated sugar	4 cups	900 mL
Raspberry flavored gelatin (jelly powder)	1 × 3 oz.	1 × 85 g

Cook beets in water until tender. Drain. Reserve juice.

Combine reserved juice, lemon juice and pectin crystals in large pot. Heat and stir on medium-high until it comes to a boil.

Stir in sugar and gelatin. Boil 6 minutes stirring occasionally. Skim off foam. Pour into hot sterilized jars to within ¼ inch (6 mm) of top. Seal. Makes 5 half pints.

Little cherry pieces are very colorful in this good conserve. A bit softer than marmalade. Also called Peach Jam.

Peaches, peeled and cut in small pieces, reserve stones	12	12
Orange, thinly peeled, white pith removed and discarded, reserve peel	1	1
Lemon with peel, cut up and seeded	1	1
Table salt	¼ tsp.	1 mL
Granulated sugar		
Bottle of maraschino cherries, drained, halved or quartered	6 oz.	170 g

Dip peaches in boiling water for ½ to 1 minute. Peel. Put peaches and stones into large pot. Grind orange peel and pulp and lemon. Add to pot.

Stir in salt. Measure bulk of fruit and add same amount of sugar. Proportion is 1 cup (250 mL) fruit mixture to 1 cup 250 mL) sugar. Boil for about 1 hour. Stir occasionally. Discard stones. Mixture will be soft but not too runny.

Add cherries just before pouring into bottles. Pour into hot sterilized jars to within ¼ inch (6 mm) of top. Seal. Makes 8 half pints.

Pictured on cover.

A favorite spread of everyone.

Strawberries, cut up	4 lbs.	1.82 kg
Granulated sugar	10 cups	2.25 L
Frozen concentrated apple juice	¼ cup	60 mL
Lemon juice, fresh or bottled	2 tbsp.	30 mL

Combine strawberries, sugar, apple juice and lemon juice in large pot. Stir over medium heat until sugar dissolves and it comes to a full rolling boil. Boil rapidly for about 20 minutes. Test a teaspoonful on a chilled saucer. It should firm up and form a light skin to be spreadable. Skim off foam. Pour into hot sterilized jars to within ¼ inch (6 mm) of top. Seal. Makes 5 pints.

MINT JELLY

A good set to this pretty jelly. Serve with lamb. Also good with ice cream.

Tart apples, such as Granny Smith, cut up	4½ lbs.	2 kg
Water	2 cups	500 mL
Chopped fresh mint, lightly packed (1 bunch)	1½ cups	375 mL
White vinegar	2 cups	500 mL
Granulated sugar, 1 cup (250 mL) to 1 cup (250 mL) juice (see Note)		
Drops of green food coloring (optional)	3-5	3-5

No need to peel or core apples. Combine apple pieces with water and mint in saucepan. Bring to a boil on medium heat. Cook until apples are mushy.

Add vinegar. Return to a boil. Boil, covered, for 5 minutes. Pour into jelly bag and strain. Measure juice into large pot.

Add the same amount of sugar as juice. Heat and stir until sugar is dissolved and a full rolling boil is reached. Add food coloring if desired. Boil rapidly for about 25 to 30 minutes, until it jells when tested. Pour into hot sterilized jars to within ¼ inch (6 mm) of top. Seal. Makes 4 half pints.

Note: Taste juice before adding sugar. If not minty enough, add 2 or 3 sprigs of mint along with sugar. Discard mint before filling jars.

Pictured on page 125.

SAVORY TOMATO JAM

Spread this on meat rather than toast, although you may want to try it on toast, too.

Ripe tomatoes	5 lbs.	2.5 kg
Grated rind of lemon	4 tsp.	20 mL
Lemon juice, fresh or bottled	½ cup	125 mL
Granulated sugar	4 cups	1 L
White vinegar	2 cups	500 mL
Ground cinnamon	2 tsp.	10 mL
Coarse (pickling) salt	1 tsp.	5 mL

(continued on next page)

Dip tomatoes into boiling water for about 1 minute until they peel easily. Peel and cut up. Place in saucepan. Bring to a boil slowly. Stir often as it boils in uncovered saucepan. Boil, uncovered, about 20 to 30 minutes until liquid is reduced.

Add lemon rind, lemon juice, sugar, vinegar, cinnamon and salt. Stir as it returns to a boil. Boil about 40 minutes, stirring often, until it thickens. Test on chilled saucer to see if it is thick enough. Pour into hot sterilized jars to within ¼ inch (6 mm) of top. Seal. Makes 4 half pints.

RASPBERRY JAM

Real raspberry jam. Dark red in color.

Raspberries, packed	4 cups	1 L
Granulated sugar	3 cups	750 mL
Lemon juice, fresh or bottled	1 tbsp.	15 mL

Place raspberries in large pot. Cover with sugar. Stir. Let stand on counter about 1 to 2 hours until berries release their juice.

Add lemon juice. Heat on low, stirring occasionally, until it begins to bubble. Simmer slowly, stirring until sugar dissolves. Increase heat to high and bring to a rolling boil. Boil hard for about 20 minutes, stirring occasionally until it thickens. Test a little on a chilled saucer to see if it is thickness of jam. Pour into hot sterilized jars to within ¼ inch (6 mm) of top. Seal. Makes 2 half pints and 1 small jar.

LOGANBERRY JAM: Use loganberries instead of raspberries.

BLACKBERRY JAM: Use blackberries instead of raspberries.

Paré Pointer

Mom told Johnny he would never get punished for something he didn't do. So why did he got into trouble for not doing his homework?

APRICOT JAM

A pretty jam. Good tasting as well!

Apricots, halved and pitted	2 lbs.	900 g
Lemon juice, fresh or bottled	¼ cup	60 mL
Pectin crystals	1 × 2 oz.	1 × 56 g
Granulated sugar	6 cups	1.35 L
Almond flavoring (optional)	¼ tsp.	1 mL

Grind apricots using coarse blade. Place in large pot.

Add lemon juice and pectin. Heat and stir on medium-high until it boils very rapidly.

Mix in sugar. Stir to dissolve. Return to a full boil. Boil hard for 4 minutes. Add almond flavoring. Skim off foam. Pour into hot sterilized jars to within ¼ inch (6 mm) of top. Seal. Makes 6 half pints.

PINCHERRY JELLY

There is no better snack than toast with this jelly. No one will mind if you don't have baking on hand.

Pincherries	3 lbs.	1.36 L
Water	3 cups	675 mL
Prepared juice	3 cups	675 mL
Granulated sugar	6½ cups	1.46 L
Liquid pectin	6 oz.	170 g

Combine pincherries and water in large pot. Heat on medium-high until it comes to a boil. Boil slowly for 15 minutes stirring occasionally. Pour berries and juice into jelly bag in bowl. Tie bag above bowl or place bag in food mill or large sieve so juice will drain into bowl.

Combine reserved juice and sugar in large pot. Stir over fairly high heat until it comes to a boil.

Stir in pectin, continuing to stir as it comes to a full rolling boil. Boil hard 1 minute. Remove from heat. Skim off foam and pour quickly into hot sterilized jars to within ¼ inch (6 mm) of top. Seal. Makes 6 half pints.

Pictured on page 143.

CHOKECHERRY JELLY: Use chokecherries instead of pincherries.

MOCK APRICOT JAM

Tasty and pretty.

Carrots, cooked and mashed	1 lb.	454 g
Granulated sugar	1 lb.	454 g
Grated rind of lemon	1	1
Lemon juice, fresh or bottled	1/4 cup	60 mL
Almond extract	1/8 tsp.	0.5 mL

Combine first 3 ingredients in large saucepan. Bring to a boil on medium heat. Boil, uncovered, for 5 minutes. Stir continually. Remove from heat. Cool to room temperature.

Add lemon juice and almond flavoring. Stir. Cool for 15 minutes. Put into containers. Cover. Store in refrigerator 8 to 10 months. May also be poured boiling hot into hot sterilized jars to within 1/4 inch (6 mm) of top and sealed. Makes 2 half pints plus 1 small jar (625 mL).

FREEZER STRAWBERRY JAM

This has the best color and the freshest flavor of all jams.

Strawberries	5 cups	1 L
Granulated sugar	4 cups	900 mL
Lemon juice, fresh or bottled	2 tbsp.	30 mL
Liquid fruit pectin	3 oz.	85 mL

Mash strawberries to yield 1³/₄ cups (400 mL). Combine with sugar in bowl. Let stand 10 minutes.

Add lemon juice and liquid pectin to fruit mixture. Stir continually for 3 minutes. Spoon into containers and cover. Leave 1 inch (2.5 cm) space at top of container to allow for expansion when frozen. Cover. Let stand for up to 24 hours at room temperature until set. Freeze. Chill jam once opened. Makes 5 half pints.

FREEZER RASPBERRY JAM: Use 2 cups (450 mL) mashed raspberries instead of strawberries.

APPLE JELLY

A mild glistening jelly that is easy to make without adding pectin.

Tart apples, such as Granny Smith	4½ lbs.	2 kg
Water	7 cups	1.58 L
Prepared juice	5 cups	1.13 L
Lemon juice, fresh or bottled	3 tbsp.	50 mL
Granulated sugar	3¾ cups	850 mL

Remove stems and blossom ends from apples. Coarsely chop apples with peel and core included. Turn into large pot. Add water. Bring to a boil on medium-high heat. Cook about 50 minutes until mushy-soft. Drain several hours or overnight in jelly bag.

Combine prepared juice and lemon juice in large pot. Add sugar. Stir on medium-high heat until it comes to a full rolling boil. Boil hard for about 40 minutes, stirring once or twice, testing for jelly stage near the end. Skim off foam if necessary. Pour into hot sterilized jars to within ¼ inch (6 mm) of top. Seal. Makes 3 half pints.

Pictured on page 89.

CRABAPPLE JELLY: Use crabapples instead of apples.

RED CURRANT JELLY

Excellent as a spread. Excellent with meat and poultry.

Red currants	8 cups	1.8 L
Water	2 cups	450 mL
Prepared juice	4 cups	900 mL
Granulated sugar	3½ cups	800 mL

Combine currants and water in large pot. Bring to a boil over medium heat. Boil gently, stirring often, for 10 to 15 minutes until currants are soft. Drain in jelly bag overnight.

Place prepared juice in large pot. Bring to a boil over medium-high heat. Boil rapidly for 5 minutes.

Stir in sugar until it dissolves. Boil hard for about 15 minutes, stirring once or twice, testing for jelling stage near the end. Pour into hot sterilized jars to within ¼ inch (6 mm) of top. Seal. Makes 3 half pints.

HOT PEPPER JELLY

This makes a greenish-colored jelly. Use red peppers to make a orange-red color. Great over a bar of cream cheese served with crackers.

Seeded, chopped green or red peppers	1½ cups	350 mL
Chopped canned jalapeño peppers	¼ cup	60 mL
White vinegar	1½ cups	350 mL
Granulated sugar	6½ cups	1.5 L
Liquid pectin	6 oz.	170 mL
Green food coloring (optional)		

Combine chopped peppers and vinegar in blender. Blend smooth. Pour into large pot.

Add sugar. Heat on medium-high and stir until sugar dissolves. Bring to a boil. Boil for 3 minutes.

Stir in pectin. Return to a full rolling boil on high. Boil hard for 1 minute. Remove from heat. Skim off foam.

Add a bit of food coloring if desired to make a stronger green. Pour into hot sterilized jars to within ¼ inch (6 mm) of top. Seal. Makes 6 half pints.

Pictured on page 53.

WHIPPED RASPBERRY JAM

Clear and fresh tasting.

Raspberries	4 cups	1 L
Granulated sugar	4 cups	1 L

Place raspberries in large pot. Using potato masher, mash well. Stir on medium heat until it comes to a boil. Boil rapidly for 2 minutes.

Add sugar. Return to a boil, stirring continually. Boil rapidly 2 minutes more. Remove from heat. Beat with electric beater for 4 minutes. Pour into hot sterilized jars to within ¼ inch (6 mm) of top. Seal. Makes 3 half pints plus 1 small jar.

Pictured on page 143.

BLUEBERRY-RHUBARB JAM

Rhubarb adds an extra interesting flavor. Recipe may be halved.

Ground rhubarb, about 2 lbs. (900 g) (see Note)	4 cups	900 mL
Ground blueberries or saskatoons, about 2 lbs. (900 g)	4 cups	900 mL
Granulated sugar	14 cups	3.15 L
Liquid pectin	6 oz.	170 mL

Combine rhubarb and blueberry pulp in large pot. Amounts of each needn't be exact as long as the total amount is 8 cups (1.8 L). Mix in sugar. Heat and stir on medium-high until sugar dissolves. Bring to a boil. Boil 5 minutes, stirring occasionally.

Add pectin. Return to a full rolling boil on high. Boil hard for 1 minute. Remove from heat. Skim off foam. Pour into hot sterilized jars to within 1/4 inch (6 mm) of top. Seal. Makes 7 1/2 pints.

Note: Cut rhubarb into short pieces before grinding.

MOCK GRAPE JELLY

This clear real grape flavor would fool anyone.

Beets, peeled and cut up	4 lbs.	1.8 kg
Water	6 cups	1.35 L
Reserved cooking water, plus water if needed	4 1/4 cups	950 mL
Packaged grape drink powder, without sugar (such as Kool Aid)	1 x 1/4 oz.	1 x 6 g
Pectin crystals	1 x 2 oz.	1 x 57 g
Salt, just a pinch		
Granulated sugar	4 cups	900 mL

Cook beets in water until tender. Drain and reserve cooking water.

Measure beet cooking water, drink powder, pectin and salt into large pot. Bring to a boil on medium-high, stirring until granules are dissolved. Boil 7 minutes, stirring occasionally.

Add sugar. Stir to dissolve. Bring to a rolling boil. Boil 1 minute. Skim off foam. Pour into hot sterilized jars to within 1/4 inch (6 mm) of top. Seal. Makes 5 half pints.

GOOSEBERRY JAM

Just the right tartness.

Granulated sugar	4 cups	1 L
Water	1 cup	250 mL
Gooseberries, tipped and stemmed, about 4 cups (1 L)	2 lbs.	1 kg

Combine sugar and water in large pot. Heat and stir on medium-high until sugar dissolves. Bring to a boil. Boil, uncovered, for 15 minutes, stirring occasionally.

Add gooseberries. Return to a boil. Boil for about 30 minutes until a small amount cools and sets on a chilled saucer. Skim off foam if needed. Pour into hot sterilized jars to within ¼ inch (6 mm) of top. Seal. Makes 4 half pints.

ZUCCHINI-PEACH JAM

A superb taste for a bargain jam.

Peeled and grated zucchini (5 to 6 medium)	6 cups	1.35 L
Granulated sugar	6 cups	1.35 L
Crushed pineapple with juice	¾ cup	175 mL
Lemon juice, fresh or bottled	½ cup	125 mL
Peach flavored gelatin (jelly powder)	2 x 3 oz.	2 x 85 g

Stir zucchini and sugar together in large pot. Heat, uncovered, on medium stirring a few times until it comes to a boil. Boil gently for 15 minutes, stirring occasionally.

Add pineapple with juice and lemon juice. Stir. Return to a boil. Boil, uncovered, for 6 minutes. Stir occasionally.

Stir in gelatin until it dissolves. Skim off foam. Pour into hot sterilized jars to within ¼ inch (6 mm) of top. Seal. Makes 8 half pints.

Pictured on page 89.

BLACK CURRANT JAM

Easy to make, especially by not topping and tailing berries.

Black currants	**2 lbs.**	**1.8 kg**
Water	**1⅓ cups**	**300 mL**
Granulated sugar	**8 cups**	**1.8 L**
Liquid pectin	**3 oz.**	**85 g**

If, after washing the currants they are fairly clean stemmed, you can either pick off remaining stems and blossom ends (tedious and time consuming) or coarsely chop in food processor without removing ends. You will never know the difference. Combine currants with water in large pot. Simmer, stirring occasionally, for about 30 minutes until skins are very tender.

Stir in sugar until it dissolves and mixture comes to a full rolling boil. Boil hard for 10 minutes. Stir once or twice.

Add pectin. Boil hard for 2 minutes. Fill hot sterilized jars to within ¼ inch (6 mm) of top. Seal. Makes about 8 half pints.

PEACH FREEZER JAM

A fresh peach taste for the middle of winter.

Peeled, pitted and mashed peaches, about 1 lb. (454 g)	**1 cup**	**250 mL**
Granulated sugar	**2¾ cups**	**625 mL**
Light corn syrup	**½ cup**	**125 mL**
Lemon juice, fresh or bottled	**1 tbsp.**	**15 mL**
Liquid fruit pectin, fresh or bottled	**3 oz.**	**85 g**

Combine peaches, sugar, syrup and lemon juice in bowl. Stir well. Let stand 10 minutes.

Add pectin. Stir until sugar is dissolved. Pour into small containers, leaving 1 inch (2.5 cm) headroom. Cover. Freeze. Store container in use in refrigerator up to 1 month. Makes 3½ cups (800 mL).

PEACH-STRAWBERRY JAM: Use half mashed peaches and half mashed strawberries.

PARSLEY FLAKES

It's easy to preserve this popular home-grown herb.

Fresh parsley sprigs

Put about 5 bushy sprigs of parsley in a circle on a paper towel in microwave oven. Cover with second paper towel. It's better to dry in small quantities. Heat on high for 2 minutes. Check parsley. If moist, heat 1 minute more. Heat for 30 second intervals if needed. Cool on wire rack. Parsley should be dry and brittle. When crushing for storage, discard heavy stems. Store in small jars or any small containers.

CELERY FLAKES: Use leaves from celery heads.

PARTY SAUSAGE

What you see is what you get. No filler added. Wonderful warm, delicious cold. An anytime hit.

Curing salt (not coarse/pickling salt)	3 tbsp.	45 mL
Liquid smoke	2 tbsp.	30 mL
Mustard seed	1 tbsp.	15 mL
Onion salt	2 tsp.	10 mL
Garlic salt	1 tsp.	5 mL
Water	½ cup	125 mL
Lean ground beef	6 lbs.	2.72 kg

Measure first 5 spices into large bowl. Mix. Add water. Stir well.

Mix in half the meat first, then add and mix in second half. Shape into 5 rolls, about 2 inches (5 cm) in diameter. Roll snugly in foil. Refrigerate for 24 hours. Poke holes on top and bottom of foil. Arrange on broiler pan or tray. Cook in 300°F (150°C) oven for 2 hours. Cool. Wrap over foil to freeze for up to 6 months. Makes about 4¼ pounds (2 kg).

Pictured on page 53.

HAM JERKY

With a touch of mustard.

Fully cooked boneless ham	2 lbs.	900 g
Prepared mustard	½ cup	125 mL
Water	½ cup	125 mL

Trim fat from ham. Slice meat across the grain into ¼ inch (6 mm) thick pieces. Cut slices into strips about 1½ inch (4 cm) in width, making strips as long as possible.

Stir mustard and water together in small bowl. Place ham strips and mustard mixture in plastic bag. Gently press and squeeze until all strips are covered. Tie bag and store in refrigerator overnight. Place wire cooling racks in large pans with sides. Remove ham strips, rub over edge of bowl to remove excess marinade, place close together on racks. Dry in 150°F (65°C) oven for 7 to 8 hours, depending on thickness. Turn strips over at half time. Change position of pans at half time. Strips should feel hard and dry. Store in freezer for long-term storage.

Pictured on page 53.

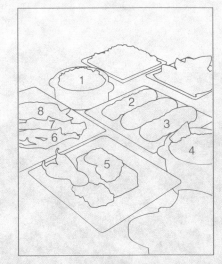

Card Mugs Courtesy Of:
Le Gnome

Card Table/Chairs Courtesy Of:
Dufferin Game Room Store

China Courtesy Of:
Call The Kettle Black

An all-time favorite flavor. A lunch box treat that can be made all year.

Tart apples, peeled, cored and cut up	1½ lbs.	680 g
Water	¼ cup	60 mL
Prepared apple purée	2 cups	450 mL
Honey or granulated sugar	1-4 tbsp.	15-60 mL
Ground cinnamon (optional)	¼ tsp.	1 mL

Cook apples in water until barely tender. Drain. Run through blender to smooth.

Place purée in bowl. Add honey and cinnamon to taste. Stir well. Line 10 x 15 inch (25 x 38 cm) jelly roll pan with plastic wrap, using 2 sheets crosswise fashion so as to have plenty of overhang. Spread purée mixture over plastic. Dry in 150°F (65°C) oven overnight, or for 8 to 10 hours during the day, until dry and leathery. It will be stiff enough to pull off plastic wrap. May be turned to dry other side a bit. It should be pliable and stretch a bit as it is torn. Roll up with plastic to store in airtight container or freeze.

Note: A 12 x 18 inch (30 x 45 cm) pan may he used for 2½ cups (575 mL) purée.

Pictured on cover.

APRICOT LEATHER

Apricots, halved and pitted	1 lb.	454 g
Crushed pineapple, drained	½ cup	125 mL
Lemon juice, fresh or bottled	1 tbsp.	15 mL
Honey or granulated sugar	1-4 tbsp.	15-60 mL

Purée and measure. No cooking required. Dry as for Apple Leather.

Pictured on cover.

KIWIFRUIT LEATHER: Purée about 1½ pounds (680 g). Measure. Sweeten to taste. No cooking required. Dry as above.

Pictured on cover.

STRAWBERRY LEATHER: Purée about 2½ cups (600 mL) strawberries. Measure and sweeten to taste. No cooking required. Dry as above.

Pictured on page 35.

BEEF JERKY

Good stuff!

Soy sauce	⅓ cup	75 mL
Brown sugar	3 tbsp.	50 mL
Worcestershire sauce	2 tsp.	10 mL
Onion powder	¼ tsp.	1 mL
Ground ginger	¼ tsp.	1 mL
Garlic powder	¼ tsp.	1 mL
Liquid smoke	¼ tsp.	1 mL
Table salt	½ tsp.	2 mL
Lean beef, top round, fat removed, about 1 inch (2.5 cm) thick (see Note)	1 lb.	454 g

Mix first 8 ingredients in bowl. Set aside.

Cut meat across the grain into ⅛ to ¼ inch (3 to 6 mm) thick slices. Do not cut too thick or center won't dry. Using partially frozen meat makes this easier to do. Add beef strips to ingredients in bowl. Stir to coat. Cover. Let stand in refrigerator overnight. Draw strips across edge of bowl to remove excess marinade. Place wire cooling racks in baking pans with sides. Arrange single layer of beef strips on racks. Put in 150°F (65°C) oven for 7 to 8 hours. Turn strips over and rearrange pans at half time. Fills 2 tall, narrow jars. Freeze for long-term storage.

Note: You can ask your butcher to slice thin layers of meat from top round. Then all you need to do is cut into strips.

SMOKY JERKY

An added dimension to this great chew.

Top round beef steak, cut in ¼ inch (6 mm) thick slices, fat removed	2 lbs.	900 g
Water	1 cup	225 mL
Worcestershire sauce	2 tsp.	10 mL
Table salt	2 tsp.	10 mL
Pepper	1 tsp.	5 mL
Onion salt	1 tsp.	5 mL
Garlic salt	1 tsp.	5 mL
Liquid smoke	½ tsp.	2 mL

(continued on next page)

Trim all fat from meat. Cut slices into 1½ inch (3.5 cm) wide strips, as long as possible.

Mix all remaining ingredients in small bowl until salt dissolves. Turn into plastic bag. Add beef strips. Push and squeeze gently to coat all pieces. Tie securely. Store in refrigerator overnight. Draw strips across edge of bowl to remove excess marinade. Arrange strips close together in single layer on wire cooling racks in baking sheets with sides. Dry in 150°F (65°C) oven for 7 to 8 hours. Turn slices over and reposition pans at half time. Strips should feel dry and hard, but pliable enough to bend. Cool. Store in airtight containers in cool location or in refrigerator. Freeze for long-term storage. Makes about 1 pound (454 g).

SIMPLE JERKY: Marinate beef strips in your favorite barbecue sauce. Draw strips across edge of bowl to remove excess sauce. Proceed as above.

Pictured on page 53.

CHICKEN SAUSAGE

A peppery flavored sausage. Slice thinly for making your own sandwiches or appetizers.

Table salt	2 tsp.	10 mL
Pepper	¾ tsp.	4 mL
Thyme	¼ tsp.	1 mL
Sage	¼ tsp.	1 mL
Cayenne pepper	¼ tsp.	1 mL
Water	1 tbsp.	15 mL
Ground fresh chicken or turkey	**3 lbs.**	**1.36 kg.**

Stir first 6 ingredients together in large bowl.

Add ground chicken. Mix. Shape into 3 rolls, 2 inches (5 cm) in diameter. Roll snugly in foil and store 24 hours in refrigerator. Poke holes in top and bottom of foil. Arrange on broiler pan or tray. Cook in 300°F (150°C) oven for 2 hours. Wrap well. Store in freezer for up to 6 months. Makes 2 pounds (900 g).

Pictured on page 53.

TURKEY JERKY

A necessity for hunting trips or a good take-along anywhere.

Boneless turkey breast	**2 lbs.**	**900 g**
Soy sauce	**¼ cup**	**60 mL**
Water	**¼ cup**	**60 mL**
Ketchup	**2 tbsp.**	**30 mL**
Granulated sugar	**1 tbsp.**	**15 mL**
Table salt	**2 tsp.**	**10 mL**
Pepper	**½ tsp.**	**2 mL**
Onion powder	**½ tsp.**	**2 mL**
Garlic powder	**½ tsp.**	**2 mL**
Worcestershire sauce	**½ tsp.**	**2 mL**
Liquid smoke	**½ tsp.**	**2 mL**

Slice turkey ¼ inch (6 mm) thick. Cut slices into long 1½ inch (3.5 cm) wide strips.

Combine remaining ingredients in small bowl. Stir until salt dissolves. Turn into plastic bag. Add turkey strips. Squeeze gently until all pieces are coated. Tie securely. Chill in refrigerator overnight. Draw strips across edge of bowl to remove excess marinade. Arrange close together in single layer on wire cooling racks placed in baking sheets with sides. Dry in 150°F (65°C) oven for 7 to 8 hours. Turn strips over and rearrange pans at half time. Strips should feel dry and hard but will still bend. Cool. Store in jar or plastic bag in cool place or refrigerator. Freeze for long-term storage.

Pictured on page 53.

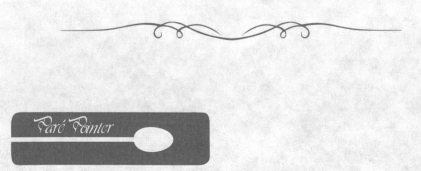

Paré Pointer

Providing you have a ham and a ballpoint you would have a pig pen.

APPLE MARMALADE

A great flavor. Good on breakfast rolls.

Tart apples, such as Granny Smith, peeled, cored and thinly sliced	4	4
Grated rind and juice of small orange	¹/₂	¹/₂
Grated rind and juice of small lemon	¹/₂	¹/₂
Water	¹/₂ cup	125 mL
Granulated sugar	2 cups	500 mL

Prepare fruit, rind and juice. Place in bowl.

Stir water and sugar in large saucepan on medium heat until mixture boils. Add fruit mixture. Return to a boil. Simmer, uncovered, stirring occasionally for about 45 minutes until fruit is clear and mixture thickens. Cool a small spoonful to room temperature on chilled saucer to see if it jells. When jelly stage is reached, fill hot sterilized jars to within ¹/₄ inch (6 mm) of top. Seal. Makes 2 half pints.

ORANGE-PINEAPPLE MARMALADE

Any time is preserving time with this easy recipe. It's a snap to make and is destined to be your favorite marmalade.

Large oranges	4	4
Water	2 cups	500 mL
Granulated sugar	4 cups	900 ml
Canned crushed pineapple with juice	2 × 14 oz.	2 × 398 mL

Grate rind from oranges. Put rind and water into saucepan. Use orange for another purpose. Bring to a boil. Cover and simmer until soft, about 5 to 10 minutes. Strain juice into saucepan.

Add sugar and crushed pineapple. Bring to a boil, stirring often. Boil rapidly for about 35 minutes, stirring 2 or 3 times, until thick enough. Cool a teaspoonful on a chilled saucer to see if it jells. Fill hot sterilized jars to within ¹/₄ inch (6 mm) of top. Seal. Makes 3 half pints and 1 small jar.

GINGER-PEAR MARMALADE

Perfect combination.

Peeled, cored and sliced pears, about 4½ lbs. (2 kg)	10 cups	2.25 L
Grated rind and juice of orange	1	1
Grated rind and juice of lemon	1	1
Granulated sugar	6 cups	1.35 L
Piece of ginger root, about 2 inch (5 cm) length, tied in double layer of cheesecloth		

Combine all ingredients in large pot. Stir. Let stand about 1 hour until pears release their juice. Heat and stir until it comes to a boil. Cook, uncovered, stirring often until pears are mushy. Cook rapidly, stirring constantly until jam stage is reached. This will take about 55 minutes. Discard spice bag. Skim if needed. Pour into hot sterilized jars to within ¼ inch (6 mm) of top. Seal. Makes 6 half pints.

PEACH-ORANGE MARMALADE

A gorgeous shade of reddish orange. Excellent flavor.

Peaches with peel, quartered and stoned	7	7
Orange, cut up and seeds removed	1	1
Maraschino cherries, pitted	⅓ cup	75 mL
Granulated sugar, amount equal to pulp		
Almond flavoring	½ tsp.	2 mL

Put peaches, orange and cherries through food grinder. Measure pulp and turn into large pot.

Add same amount of sugar as there is pulp. Add almond flavoring. Heat and stir until sugar dissolves and it comes to a boil. Boil 30 to 40 minutes, stirring occasionally, until a small spoonful cooled on a chilled saucer jells. Pour into hot sterilized jars to within ¼ inch (6 mm) of top. Seal. Makes 5 half pints.

Pictured on page 89.

ORANGE MARMALADE

Clear, dark marmalade with slender strips of orange peel throughout.

Medium oranges	6	6
Medium lemons	3	3
Water	3 cups	700 mL
Orange rind		
Lemon rind		
Water	2¼ cups	500 mL

Granulated sugar, 1 cup (250 mL)
  to 1 cup (250 mL) fruit mixture

Peel oranges and lemons very thin trying not to have any white pith on peel. Place peel in plastic bag to keep from drying. Set aside until morning. Slice oranges and lemons into saucepan. Add first amount of water. Boil gently for 2 hours. Drain in jelly bag overnight.

Cut peel with knife or scissors into fine long shreds. Put into saucepan. Add second amount of water. Boil 15 minutes until soft, stirring occasionally. Drain and measure 2 cups (450 mL) juice adding a bit of water if needed. Add to juice from jelly bag.

Mix and measure peel and juice, then place in large pot. Add same measure of sugar to pot. Stir on medium-high heat until it boils. Boil rapidly, stirring 2 or 3 times, until a bit will jell when cooled on a chilled saucer. This will take about 25 minutes. Pour into hot sterilized jars to within ¼ inch (6 mm) of top. Seal. Makes 3 half pints and 1 small jar.

GOLDEN RHUBARB MARMALADE

Good taste and texture. A hint of orange.

Chopped rhubarb	8 cups	1.8 L
Granulated sugar	10 cups	2.25 L
Oranges, put through food grinder	3	3
Lemon, put through food grinder	1	1

Combine all ingredients in large bowl. Stir. Cover and let stand overnight on counter. Turn into large pot. Bring to a boil on medium-high heat, stirring often. Boil for 30 minutes. Cool a small spoonful to room temperature on chilled saucer to see if it jells. When jelly stage is reached, fill hot sterilized jars to within ¼ inch (6 mm) of top. Seal. Makes 10 half pints.

THREE FRUIT MARMALADE

Very good flavor. Makes a large batch but may be halved. Not a real firm marmalade.

Grapefruit, cut up	½	½
Orange, quartered	1	1
Lemons, halved	1	1

Water, 3 times amount of fruit

Granulated sugar, 1½ times quantity of pulp

Remove seeds from grapefruit, orange and lemon. Put through food grinder. Measure and put into large pot.

For each 1 cup (250 mL) pulp, add 3 cups (750 mL) water. Bring to a boil, stirring occasionally. Simmer for 20 minutes. Boil rapidly, stirring 2 or 3 times, for 20 minutes. Measure quantity.

To each 1 cup (250 mL) pulp, add 1½ cups (375 mL) sugar. Return to a boil, stirring. Boil rapidly until thickened and a small amount cooled on a chilled saucer jells. This will take about 20 minutes. Pour into hot sterilized jars to within ¼ inch (6 mm) of top. Seal. Makes 5 half pints.

CARROT MARMALADE

Lots of body to this. Very pretty color.

Grated carrots, about 2 lbs. (900 g)	6 cups	1.35 L
Lemons with peel, seeded and ground	1½	1½
Oranges with peel, seeded and ground	1½	1½
Canned crushed pineapple with juice	1 cup	225 mL
Granulated sugar	6 cups	1.35 L
Table salt	½ tsp.	2 mL
Chopped maraschino cherries	⅓ cup	75 mL

Mix first 6 ingredients in large bowl. Cover and let stand overnight on counter. Transfer to large pot. Bring to a boil over medium heat, stirring frequently. Boil rapidly for 3 minutes without stirring.

Add cherries. Stir. Pour into hot sterilized jars to within ¼ inch (6 mm) of top. Seal. Makes 8 half pints.

Pictured on page 143.

ZUCCHINI MARMALADE

Economical and flavorful.

Zucchini, peeled, cut and seeded	6 lbs.	2.7 kg
Granulated sugar	12 cups	2.7 L
Oranges with peel	3	3
Lemons with peel	2	2
Crystallized ginger	2 oz.	56 g

Put zucchini through food grinder into bowl.

Pour sugar over top. Cover and let stand on counter overnight. In morning, transfer to large pot.

Cut oranges and lemons into wedges. Remove seeds. Put through food grinder. Grind ginger. Add ground ingredients to zucchini. Stir over medium heat until sugar dissolves. Bring to a boil, stirring occasionally. Boil until thickened, stirring occasionally. This will take about 1 hour 15 minutes. Cool a small spoonful on chilled saucer to see if it jells. Fill hot sterilized jars to within 1/4 inch (6 mm) of top. Seal. Makes 12 half pints.

RHUBARB MARMALADE

Good taste and texture. Orange flavor comes through.

Rhubarb, cut up	2 lbs.	900 g
Granulated sugar	2 lbs.	900 g
Oranges	1½	1½

Put rhubarb and sugar into large pot. Remove a very thin layer of orange peel with no white pith on it. Remove and discard white pith from peeled oranges. Slice peel in very thin strips. Cut strips short. Cut oranges into small pieces. Add peel and pulp to pot. Stir and bring to a boil over medium-high heat. Boil, uncovered, stirring occasionally for about 30 minutes. Cool a small spoonful on chilled saucer to see if it jells. Fill hot sterilized jars to within 1/4 inch (6 mm) of top. Seal. Makes 5 half pints.

Pictured on page 143.

PEACH-PEAR MARMALADE

A two fruit combo with cherries added for color.

Orange with peel, cut, seeded, put through grinder	1	1
Water	1 cup	250 mL
Large peaches, peeled and cut up	4	4
Pears, peeled, cored and cut up	3	3
Granulated sugar	3 cups	675 mL
Lemon juice, fresh or bottled	2 tbsp.	30 mL
Table salt	1/8 tsp.	0.5 mL
Ground ginger	1/8 tsp.	0.5 mL
Maraschino cherries, chopped	6	6

Combine ground orange and water in saucepan. Stir. Boil for 15 minutes, stirring occasionally.

Add peaches, pears, sugar, lemon juice, salt and ginger. Stir. Cook, stirring occasionally until jelling stage. This will take about 45 minutes.

Stir in cherries. Pour into hot sterilized jars to within 1/4 inch (6 mm) of top. Seal. Makes 4 half pints.

WALNUT MARMALADE

Dark colored with a lovely nutty flavor. Easy to double or triple the recipe.

Peaches, peeled and stoned	6	6
Small lemon, cut up and seeded	1	1
Chopped walnuts	1 cup	250 mL
Granulated sugar		

Put peaches, lemon and walnuts through food grinder. Measure ground bulk, then put into large pot.

Measure same amount of sugar as fruit and walnut mixture and add to pot. Stir and bring to a boil. Boil gently for 35 to 40 minutes. Test for doneness. A small mound cooled on a chilled saucer will hold its shape. Fill hot sterilized jars to within 1/4 inch (6 mm) of top. Seal. Makes 4 half pints.

A different pickle. Glistening yellow.

Ripe, firm papayas, about 5 lbs. (2.27 kg)	4	4
Granulated sugar	4 cups	900 mL
White vinegar	4 cups	900 mL
Mixed pickling spice, tied in double layer of cheesecloth	2½ tbsp.	40 mL

Peel papayas. Cut in half. Remove seeds. Cut each half in sticks, cubes or slices.

Combine sugar, vinegar and pickling spice in large saucepan. Heat and stir on medium until sugar is dissolved. Add papaya. Bring to a boil. Reduce heat. Simmer, stirring occasionally, until papaya is translucent and tender. This will take about 45 to 50 minutes. Remove spice bag. Pack jars with fruit to within 1 inch (2.5 cm) of top. Fill with syrup to within ¼ inch (6 mm) of top. Seal. Let stand 3 weeks before serving. Makes 4 half pints.

Pictured on page 107.

If you eat this with your eyes closed, you will never guess what it is.

Garlic cloves	½ lb.	250 g
Large red pepper, seeded and slivered	1	1
White vinegar	2 cups	500 mL
Granulated sugar	⅔ cup	150 mL
Mustard seed	½ tsp.	2 mL
Celery seed	½ tsp.	2 mL

Peel garlic. Leave small cloves whole. Cut large cloves in half. Combine with red pepper.

Measure vinegar and sugar into saucepan. Place mustard seed and celery seed into cotton bag. Tie. Add to saucepan. Heat on medium-high, stirring frequently, until it boils. Boil 5 minutes. Add garlic and red pepper. Return to a boil. Boil 5 minutes more. Discard spice bag. Fill hot sterilized jars with garlic and red peppers to within 1 inch (2.5 cm) of top. Fill with hot brine to within ¼ inch (6 mm) of top. Seal. Let stand several weeks before serving. Makes 2 half pints.

Pictured on page 107.

PICKLED BEETS

A different twist to these. Recipe may be halved.

Small beets	10 lbs.	4.5 kg
Boiling water		
Cider vinegar	4¹/₂ cups	1.1 L
Water	2 cups	500 mL
Granulated sugar	3³/₄ cups	850 mL
Table salt	2¹/₂ tsp.	12 mL
Mustard seed	1¹/₄ tsp.	6 mL
Celery seed	1¹/₄ tsp.	6 mL

Leave about 1 inch (2.5 cm) tops on beets. Cook in boiling water until tender. Drain. Pour cold water over beets. Rub off skin with your hands. Fill quart or pint jars to within 1 inch (2.5 cm) of top. Cut any that seem too large.

Combine vinegar, second amount of water, sugar and salt in large saucepan.

Tie mustard and celery seed in cotton bag. Add to saucepan. Bring to a boil. Cook slowly for about 15 minutes, stirring occasionally. Remove bag. Pour syrup over beets to within ¹/₄ inch (6 mm) of top. Seal. Let stand 3 weeks before using. Makes about 6 quarts.

Pictured on page 107.

A budget is when you worry about money before you spend it as well as after you spend it.

Very good and very colorful in a yellowish sauce. Excellent choice.

Chopped unpeeled cucumbers, fairly chunky	2 cups	500 mL
Chopped onions, fairly chunky	2 cups	500 mL
Small gherkin-type cucumbers, whole or halved crosswise	2 cups	500 mL
Small white pearl onions, whole	2 cups	500 mL
Coarse (pickling) salt	1 cup	250 mL
Water	1 cup	250 mL
Celery head, chopped (see Note)	1/2	1/2
Small red peppers, seeded and chopped	2	2
Tart apples, peeled, cored and chopped	2	2
SAUCE		
Granulated sugar	3 1/2 cups	825 mL
White vinegar	3 cups	750 mL
Mustard seed	4 1/3 tbsp.	65 mL
All-purpose flour	6 tbsp.	100 mL
Dry mustard powder	1 1/2 tbsp.	25 mL
Turmeric	2 tsp.	10 mL
Water	3/4 cup	175 mL

Combine first amounts of cucumber and onion and second amounts of cucumber and onion in large bowl.

In medium bowl measure salt and water. Stir well. Pour over cucumber mixture. Mix well. Cover and let stand on counter overnight. Drain. Rinse well with water. Drain.

Add celery, red pepper and apple. Stir. Set aside.

Sauce: Using large pot, combine sugar, vinegar and mustard seed. Stir over medium-high heat until it boils. Add all prepared vegetables. Return to a boil, stirring frequently.

Stir flour, mustard and turmeric together in small bowl. Mix in water until smooth and free of lumps. Stir into boiling vegetables until it returns to a boil. Boil 10 minutes on medium heat, stirring constantly. Pour into hot sterilized jars to within 1/4 inch (6 mm) of top. Seal. Let stand 2 weeks before serving. Makes 6 pints.

Note: Chop ribs, using half the ribs of a whole stalk or head of celery.

Pictured on cover.

WATERMELON RIND PICKLES

A tasty conversational pickle.

Large watermelon, 9 to 10 lbs. (4 to 4.5 kg)	1	1
Water to cover		
Water	2 cups	500 mL
Cider vinegar	3 cups	750 mL
Granulated sugar	6 cups	1.5 L
Cinnamon sticks, broken up	3	3
Whole cloves	1½ tsp.	7 mL

Cut watermelon in half. Place flesh side down. Cut into 1 inch (2.5 cm) slices. Cut pink flesh away from rind leaving a bit here and there for color. Peel off green skin with a potato peeler. Cut white rind into 1 inch (2.5 cm) pieces. You should have 4 pounds (1.8 kg). Place in large pot.

Add water to cover. Bring to a boil over medium heat. Cover and cook slowly about 15 minutes until tender crisp. Drain. Turn out rind into bowl.

Measure second amount of water, vinegar and sugar into large pot. Tie cinnamon and cloves in double layer of cheesecloth and add. Bring to a boil over medium-high heat, stirring often. Boil 5 minutes. Add rind. Return to a boil. Reduce heat. Simmer, uncovered, stirring occasionally, for about 1 hour until rind is clear looking. Remove spice bag. Fill hot sterilized jars with rind to within 1 inch (2.5 cm) of top. Fill with brine to within ¼ inch (6 mm) of top. Seal. Let stand 3 weeks before serving. Makes 3 pints.

Pictured on page 71.

Paré Pointer

One light bulb said to another light bulb "I want you watts and watts."

Triple this good old recipe so you have some for offspring and friends.

Green tomatoes, sliced	5⅓ lbs.	2.5 kg
Onions, cut up	1½ lbs.	680 g
Coarse (pickling) salt	⅓ cup	75 mL
Granulated sugar	3⅓ cups	750 mL
Mixed pickling spice, tied in double layer of cheesecloth	4½ tbsp.	85 mL
Turmeric	2 tsp.	10 mL
White vinegar	2 cups	450 mL

Layer tomatoes with onion and salt in large pot. Cover and let stand on counter overnight. Drain.

Add remaining ingredients. Vinegar should just be a bit visible. Too much will make excessive juice. Heat and stir until sugar dissolves. Bring to a boil. Simmer, uncovered, for 2 hours, stirring occasionally. More turmeric can be added for color and more sugar can be added for taste. In order to obtain an accurate taste, cool a spoonful and then sample. Pour into hot sterilized jars to within ¼ inch (6 mm) of top. Seal. Makes 4 pints.

Pictured on page 107.

Paré Pointer

If his mother comes from Iceland and his father comes from Cuba, does that make him an ice cube?

PICCALILLI

A very tasty use for green tomatoes.

Green tomatoes, chopped	3 lbs.	1.5 kg
Small green pepper, chopped	1	1
Onions, chopped	1½ lbs.	750 g
Coarse (pickling) salt	½ cup	125 mL
White vinegar	3 cups	750 mL
Granulated sugar	3 cups	750 mL
Mixed pickling spice, tied in double layer of cheesecloth	1 tbsp.	15 mL
Mustard seed	1 tsp.	5 mL

Mix first 4 ingredients in bowl. Cover. Let stand on counter overnight. Drain well, pressing to remove juice.

Combine vinegar, sugar, pickling spice and mustard seed in large pot. Add drained vegetables. Bring to a boil, stirring frequently. Allow just to simmer, uncovered, about 5 minutes until vegetables are half done. Discard spice bag. Pour into hot sterilized jars to within ¼ inch (6 mm) of top. Seal. Makes 5 pints.

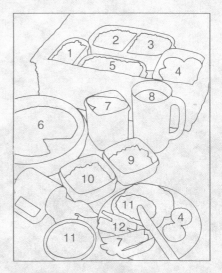

All white pickles for a different look.

Medium cucumbers, peeled	**5**	**5**
Cauliflower florets	**2 cups**	**500 mL**
Small white pearl onions, peeled, whole	**4 cups**	**1 L**
Water	**8 cups**	**2 L**
Coarse (pickling) salt	**½ cup**	**125 mL**
White vinegar	**2 cups**	**500 mL**
Water	**1 cup**	**250 mL**
BRINE		
Granulated sugar	**3 cups**	**750 mL**
White vinegar	**1½ cups**	**375 mL**
Water	**1¼ cups**	**300 mL**
Mixed pickling spice	**1¼ tsp.**	**6 mL**

Cut cucumbers in half crosswise. Cut each piece in half lengthwise. Now cut each ¼ cucumber into 4 pieces. Place in large bowl. Add cauliflower. Immerse a few onions at a time in boiling water for 20 to 30 seconds. Peel. Add to bowl.

Stir water and salt together well. Pour over vegetables. Cover and let stand on counter overnight. Drain. Turn into large pot.

Add vinegar and water. Bring to a boil, stirring often. Cook for 15 minutes, uncovered, stirring occasionally. Drain.

Brine: Combine sugar, vinegar and water in saucepan. Tie pickling spice in double layer of cheesecloth. Add. Stir. Bring to a boil. Boil 1 minute. Discard spice bag. Pack semi-cooled vegetables into hot sterilized jars, leaving 1 inch (2.5 cm) at top. Fill with brine to within ¼ inch (6 mm) of top. Seal. Let stand 3 weeks before serving. Makes 3½ pints.

Pictured on page 107.

Paré Pointer

She is so overweight that she's living beyond her seams.

SWEET MUSTARD PICKLES

Very good. Yellow with green bits showing. Recipe may be halved.

Cauliflower, cut in florets	1	1
Small cucumbers, whole or cut	4 cups	900 mL
Large cucumbers, cut in small pieces	4 cups	900 mL
Large onions, sliced	4 cups	900 mL
Small white pearl onions, peeled, whole	2 lbs.	900 g
Red peppers, seeded and cut in small pieces	3	3
Green peppers, seeded and cut in small pieces	2	2
Coarse (pickling) salt	1 cup	250 mL
Water	12 cups	3 L
Granulated sugar	5 cups	1.25 L
Water	1½ cups	375 mL
All-purpose flour	1 cup	250 mL
Dry mustard	¼ cup	60 mL
Turmeric	1 tbsp.	15 mL
Mustard seed	1 tbsp.	15 mL
Celery seed	1 tbsp.	15 mL
White vinegar	4½ cups	1.13 L

Put first 7 ingredients into large bowl.

Sprinkle with salt. Pour first amount of water over salt. Cover. Let stand on counter overnight.

Drain vegetables. Transfer to large pot. Add sugar and second amount of water. Heat on medium until boiling. Stir often.

Put last 6 ingredients into medium bowl. Mix into a paste. Stir into boiling vegetables. Continue to stir until it returns to boiling. Boil slowly 30 minutes, uncovered, stirring occasionally. Pour into hot sterilized jars to within ¼ inch (6 mm) of top. Seal. Makes 10 pints.

Pictured on page 107.

A great barbecue treat. Use as an extra on the condiment tray.

Small white pearl onions	**8 cups**	**2 L**
Boiling water to cover		
Boiling water	**8 cups**	**2 L**
Coarse (pickling) salt	**1 cup**	**250 mL**
BRINE		
Granulated sugar	**2 cups**	**500 mL**
White vinegar	**2 cups**	**500 mL**
Water	**1½ cups**	**375 mL**
Mixed pickling spice, tied in double	**2 tbsp.**	**30 mL**
layer of cheesecloth		

Cover onions with first amount of boiling water in large bowl. Cover and let stand 3 to 4 minutes. Drain. Rinse with cold water. Peel.

Mix second amount of boiling water and salt. Pour over onions in bowl. Cover. Let stand on counter overnight. Drain. Rinse with water and drain again.

Brine: Combine all 4 ingredients in large saucepan. Bring to a boil, stirring often. Boil 5 minutes. Discard spice bag. Add onions. Return to a boil. Fill hot sterilized jars with onions to within 1 inch (2.5 cm) of top. Pour brine in jars to within ¼ inch (6 mm) of top. Seal. Let stand 3 weeks before serving. Makes 4 pints.

Pictured on page 107.

Paré Pointer

All little pixies use elf-rising flour.

PICKLED SNOW PEAS

Not the flavor you expect from this vegetable. Really attractive on a condiment tray.

Garlic clove, per pint	1	1
Head of dill, per pint	1	1
Snow peas, per pint	5 oz.	140 g
BRINE		
Water	4 cups	1 L
White vinegar	2 cups	500 mL
Coarse (pickling) salt	5 tbsp.	75 mL

Place garlic and dill in each hot sterilized pint jar. Pack with snow peas to within 1 inch (2.5 cm) of top.

Brine: Combine water, vinegar and salt in saucepan. Bring to a boil, stirring until salt dissolves. Fill jars with boiling brine to within ¼ inch (6 mm) of top. Seal. Let stand 3 to 4 weeks before serving. Makes enough brine for about 4 pints.

Pictured on page 107.

SPICED CUCUMBER RINGS

Spicy and very economical. Serve with meat.

White vinegar	1 cup	250 mL
Water	1 cup	250 mL
Granulated sugar	4 cups	1 L
Cinnamon sticks, 3 inches (7.5 cm) each in length	3	3
Whole cloves	1 tsp.	5 mL
Red food coloring	1 tsp.	5 mL
Large cucumbers	5 lbs.	2.27 kg

Combine first 6 ingredients in large saucepan. Heat, stirring occasionally until sugar dissolves.

Cut cucumbers in half crosswise. Hollow out each half, removing seeds. Peel. Slice into ½ inch (12 mm) rings. Add to saucepan. Bring to a boil. Simmer, uncovered, for about 50 minutes. Stir more often at first until rings shrink in size enough to all be covered with liquid. Spoon rings into hot sterilized jars. Fill with liquid to within ¼ inch (6 mm) of top. Seal. Makes 2 pints.

When thinning your rows of carrots, they will be perfect for this crunchy pickle.

Head of dill, per pint	1	1
Small garlic clove, per pint	1	1
Small whole carrots or larger ones cut in fingers to fill 1 pint		
Coarse (pickling) salt, per pint	1 tbsp.	15 mL
Boiling white vinegar, per pint	¼ cup	60 mL
Boiling water to fill jar		

In bottom of hot sterilized pint jar, place head of dill and garlic.

Fill with carrot sticks to within 1 inch (2.5 cm) of top.

Measure salt over carrots. Add vinegar. Fill with water to within ¼ inch (6 mm) of top. Seal tightly. Let stand 6 weeks before using. Makes as many pints as you wish.

Pictured on page 71.

The judge found him not guilty due to a lack of evidence. The grateful prisoner said "Thank you. Does that mean I can keep the money?"

SUPER DILLS

The name says it all.

BRINE

Water	**12 cups**	**2.7 L**
White vinegar (7% is best)	**4 cups**	**900 mL**
Granulated sugar	**1 cup**	**250 mL**
Coarse (picking) salt	**1 cup**	**250 mL**
Mixed pickling spice, tied in double layer of cheesecloth	**2 tsp.**	**10 mL**
Garlic clove, per quart	**1**	**1**
Heads of dill, 3 inch (7.5 cm) stems intact, per quart	**2**	**2**
Small cucumbers	**8 lbs.**	**3.63 kg**

Brine: Combine first 5 ingredients in large pot. Stir and bring to a boil. Boil 3 to 5 minutes.

Pack hot sterilized jars with garlic, dill and cucumbers to within 1 inch (2.5 cm) of top. Fill with boiling brine to within ¼ inch (6 mm) of top. Seal. Let stand 4 to 5 weeks before serving. Makes 8 quarts.

Pictured on page 71.

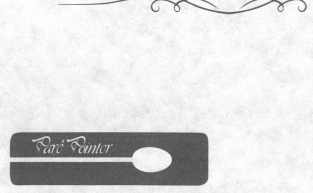

Is a string instrument player a high strung violinist?

This works well if you want to do one bottle at a time.

Heads of dill, per quart	2	2
Garlic cloves, per quart	1-2	1-2
Small pickling cucumbers		
BRINE		
Water	**1½ cups**	**375 mL**
White vinegar	**½ cup**	**125 mL**
Coarse (pickling) salt	**1½ tbsp.**	**22 mL**

Place heads of dill and garlic in hot sterilized quart jar. Fill with small cucumbers to within 1 inch (2.5 cm) of top.

Brine: Combine water, vinegar and salt in saucepan. Bring to a boil. Pour over cucumbers to within ¼ inch (6 mm) of top with boiling vinegar. Seal. Makes 1 quart.

Pictured on cover.

FAMILY DILL PICKLES: Use the following proportions: 14 cups (3.15 L) water, 2 cups (500 mL) white vinegar, 1 cup (250 mL) coarse (pickling) salt and 1 tbsp. (15 mL) mixed pickling spice tied in double layer of cheesecloth. Boil about 5 minutes and pour over cucumbers in jars. Use 2 heads of dill per quart. Let stand 4 weeks before serving.

Now that he's turned into a good handball player, he's full of under-handed tactics

PEACH PICKLES

Pretty and very appetizing.

Ripe, firm peaches	4 lbs.	1.82 kg
Boiling water		
Granulated sugar	4 cups	1 L
White vinegar	2 cups	500 mL
Cinnamon sticks, broken up	2	2
Whole cloves	20	20

Dip peaches in boiling water one at a time for 30 seconds. Run under cold water. Peel. Repeat for other peaches. Cut into 4 or 6 wedges each.

Pour sugar and vinegar into saucepan. Tie spices in double layer of cheesecloth. Add. Bring to a boil. Cover. Boil slowly for 5 minutes. Add peaches. Cook, covered, for about 5 minutes until soft. Discard spice bag. Pack peaches into hot sterilized jars to within 1 inch (2.5 cm) of top. Fill jars with syrup to within 1/4 inch (12 mm) of top. Seal. Makes 4 pints.

Pictured on page 107.

DILLY BEANS

Do these one jar or more at a time. Increase brine proportion as needed.

Green beans or wax beans, per pint	2 cups	500 mL
Boiling water		
Head of dill, per pint	1	1
Garlic clove, per pint	1/2	1/2
Cider vinegar	1 cup	250 mL
Water	1 cup	250 mL
Coarse (pickling) salt	1 1/2 tsp.	7 mL

Place beans in large pot of boiling water. Return to a boil. Boil 2 minutes. Drain. Rinse in cold water.

Put 1 head of dill and 1 garlic clove into each hot sterilized pint jar. Pack with beans to within 1 inch (2.5 cm) of top.

In large saucepan, combine vinegar, water and salt. Stir and bring to a boil. Pour over beans to within 1/4 inch (6 mm) of top. Seal. Makes as many jars as you wish.

Beans are in a yellow, creamy mustard sauce.

Yellow wax beans, cut in 1 inch (2.5 cm) lengths	2 lbs.	1 kg
Boiling water	4 cups	1 L
White vinegar	3 cups	750 mL
Brown sugar	1 cup	250 mL
Granulated sugar	1¼ cups	300 mL
All-purpose flour	½ cup	125 mL
Dry mustard powder	2 tbsp.	30 mL
Turmeric	1 tbsp.	15 mL
Celery seed	1 tsp.	5 mL
Mustard seed	½ tsp.	2 mL
Table salt	1 tsp.	5 mL
White vinegar	1 cup	250 mL

Cook beans in boiling water until just tender. Drain well.

Heat first amount of vinegar in large pot until it boils.

Measure next 8 ingredients into bowl. Stir well. Gradually stir in remaining vinegar to make a smooth paste. Stir into boiling vinegar until it returns to a boil and thickens. Add beans. Stir gently. Return to a boil. Fill hot sterilized jars to within ¼ inch (6 mm) of top. Seal. Makes 4 pints.

Pictured on page 125.

Paré Pointer

He is dumb like a fox. He managed to catch the town beauty that the wolf had been chasing for months.

CURRY PICKLES

This good pickle will be light or dark depending on how much curry you use.

Peeled, sliced cucumber 2½ lbs. (1.12 kg)	8 cups	2 L
Thinly sliced onion	2 cups	500 mL
Coarse (pickling) salt	1 tbsp.	15 mL
White vinegar	2½ cups	625 mL
Granulated sugar	2 cups	500 mL
Curry powder	2 tsp.	10 mL
Pepper	¼ tsp.	1 mL

Place cucumber, onion and salt in large bowl. Stir. Cover and let stand on counter overnight. Drain. Rinse with cold water. Drain again well.

Combine vinegar, sugar, curry powder and pepper in large pot. Stir. Bring to a boil, stirring occasionally. Add cucumber mixture. Return to a boil. Pack vegetables into hot sterilized jars to within 1 inch (2.5 cm) of top. Fill with brine to within ¼ inch (6 mm) of top. Seal. Makes 3 pints.

Pictured on page 107.

MILLION DOLLAR PICKLES

Very colorful. Easy to double.

Thinly sliced cucumber with peel	6 cups	1.5 L
Coarse (pickling) salt	3 tbsp.	50 mL
Water	2 cups	500 mL
White vinegar, almost to top of cucumber		
Sliced onion	2 cups	500 mL
Small green peppers, seeded and chopped	2	2
Granulated sugar	3 cups	750 mL
Turmeric	1 tsp.	5 mL
Chopped pimiento	4½ oz.	127 g

(continued on next page)

Place cucumber in large bowl.

Stir salt into 2 cups (500 mL) water until dissolved. Pour over cucumber. Add more water to cover. Cover and let stand overnight on counter. Drain and turn into large pot.

Add vinegar, onion, peppers, sugar and turmeric. Stir. Heat on medium-high, uncovered, stirring often until mixture just starts to boil.

Stir in pimiento. Using slotted spoon or sieve, pack hot sterilized jars with vegetables to within 1 inch (2.5 cm) of top. Fill with hot syrup to within 1/4 inch (6 mm) of top. Seal. Makes 4 pints.

Pictured on cover.

PICKLED PEPPERS

Adds gorgeous color to a condiment tray. Peter Piper would certainly approve.

Yellow, green and red peppers (mixed)	3 lbs.	1.36 kg
BRINE		
White vinegar	4 cups	900 mL
Granulated sugar	2 cups	450 mL
Coarse (pickling) salt	2 tsp.	10 mL
Boiling water		

Cut peppers in half lengthwise. Remove seeds. Cut into long strips 1/2 inch (12 mm) wide. Pack into sterilized jars to within 1 inch (2.5 cm) of top, using 1/3 of each color.

Brine: Combine vinegar, sugar and salt. Stir. Bring to a boil.

Pour boiling water over pepper in jars. Let stand 5 minutes. Drain. Fill jars with brine to within 1/4 inch (6 mm) of top. Seal. Let stand 3 weeks before using. Makes 4 pints.

Pictured on cover.

BREAD AND BUTTER PICKLES

Include these in sandwiches or burgers or serve on the side.

Sliced cucumbers with peel, ⅛ inch (3mm) thick	16 cups	3.6 L
Medium onions, thinly sliced	6	6
Large red pepper, seeded and slivered	1	1
Large green pepper, seeded and slivered	1	1
Coarse (pickling) salt	½ cup	125 mL
Granulated sugar	5 cups	1.13 L
Mustard seed	2 tbsp.	30 mL
Turmeric	1 tsp.	5 mL
Celery seed	1½ tsp.	7 mL
White vinegar	3 cups	675 mL

Place cucumber into large bowl. Add onion, red pepper, green pepper and salt. Cover and let stand on counter 3 hours. Drain well.

Combine last 5 ingredients in large pot. Heat on medium-high, stirring occasionally, until mixture boils. Add vegetables. Heat until it just reaches a boil. Using slotted spoon or sieve, fill hot sterilized jars with vegetables to within 1 inch (2.5 cm) of top. Pour hot syrup over vegetables to within ¼ inch (6 mm) of top. Seal. Makes 6 to 7 pints.

SWEET MIXED PICKLES

This short version takes only six days.

Small gherkin-type cucumbers	12 cups	2.7 L
Small white pearl onions, peeled	4 cups	900 mL
Medium cauliflower head, separated into small florets	1	1
FIRST BRINE		
Cold water	5 cups	1.3 L
Coarse (pickling) salt	½ cup	125 mL
Cold water to cover		
SECOND BRINE		
White vinegar	4 cups	900 mL
Granulated sugar	4 cups	900 mL
Celery seed	2 tbsp.	30 mL
Whole allspice	2 tbsp.	30 mL

(continued on next page)

Combine first 3 ingredients in large bowl.

First Brine: Stir first amount of water and salt together. Pour over vegetables to cover. Make more brine if necessary. Let stand 3 days, stirring each day. Drain well.

Cover vegetables with second amount of water. Let stand 3 days. Stir each day. Drain well.

Second Brine: Bring all 4 ingredients to a boil, stirring frequently. Add vegetables. Return just to the boiling point. Using a sieve and slotted spoon, pack vegetables in hot sterilized jars to within 1 inch (2.5 cm) of top. Fill with brine to within ¼ inch (6 mm) of top. Seal. Makes 4 quarts.

Pictured on cover.

SWEET PICKLED BEETS

Sweet and spicy.

Beets	2 lbs.	1 kg
Water to cover		
BRINE		
White vinegar	1½ cups	375 mL
Water	½ cup	125 mL
Granulated sugar	2 cups	500 mL
Table salt	½ tsp.	2 mL
Mixed pickling spice, tied in double layer of cheesecloth	1 tbsp.	15 mL

Cook beets in first amount of water until tender. Cool until they can be handled. Peel and cut up. Pack into hot sterilized jars to within 1 inch (2.5 cm) of top.

Brine: Bring vinegar, water, sugar and salt to a boil over medium heat in saucepan. Remove from heat.

Swish pickling spice bag around in brine for 30 seconds. Remove bag. Pour brine over beets to fill jar to within ¼ inch (6 mm) of top. Seal. Serve chilled. Makes 2 pints.

GHERKINS

Always a hit with the youngsters.

Water	10 cups	2.25 L
Coarse (pickling) salt	¾ cup	175 mL
Tiny cucumbers, smaller the better, with peel	8 cups	1.8 L
BRINE		
Granulated sugar	1¾ cups	400 mL
Water	1 cup	225 mL
White vinegar	3 cups	675 mL
Mixed pickling spice, tied in double layer of cheesecloth	1 tbsp.	15 mL

Heat and stir water and pickling salt in large pot until salt dissolves. Remove from heat. Cool.

Add cucumbers. Cover and let stand overnight. Drain.

Brine: Combine all 4 ingredients in large pot. Bring to a boil, stirring until sugar dissolves. Boil 10 minutes. Add cucumbers. Return to a boil. Boil 2 minutes more. Discard spice bag. Remove cucumbers with slotted spoon or sieve and pack into hot sterilized jars to within 1 inch (2.5 cm) of top. Fill with brine to within ¼ inch (6 mm) of top. Seal. Makes 3 to 4 pints.

NETHERLANDS PICKLES

Attractive, light colored pickles. Easy to double.

Cucumbers	2½ lbs.	1.15 kg
Coarsely chopped onion	2 cups	500 mL
Cauliflower florets, bite-size pieces	2 cups	500 mL
Coarse (pickling) salt	¼ cup	60 mL
Water	4 cups	900 mL
White vinegar	1 cup	250 mL
Granulated sugar	1 cup	250 mL
Mustard seed	½ tsp.	2 mL
Celery seed	½ tsp.	2 mL
Turmeric	¼ tsp.	1 mL

(continued on next page)

Peel and seed cucumbers. Cut in bite size chunks into large bowl. Add onion, cauliflower and salt. Stir. Cover and let stand on counter overnight. Drain well. Transfer vegetables to large pot.

Add water. Cover. Bring to a boil on medium-high heat, stirring once or twice. Cook 10 minutes. Drain.

Combine next 5 ingredients in another large pot. Stir. Bring to a boil on medium-high heat. Pack hot sterilized jars with vegetables to within 1 inch (2.5 cm) of top. Fill with hot brine to within ¼ inch (6 mm) of top. Seal. Makes 1½ pints.

ZUCCHINI PICKLES

An excellent way to use zucchini.

Thinly sliced zucchini with peel	**6 cups**	**1.5 L**
Medium onions, thinly sliced	**2**	**2**
Coarse (pickling) salt	**3 tbsp.**	**50 mL**
Granulated sugar	**2 cups**	**500 mL**
Mustard seed	**2 tsp.**	**10 mL**
Celery seed	**2 tsp.**	**10 mL**
Turmeric	**1 tsp.**	**5 mL**
White vinegar	**1¼ cups**	**300 mL**

Zucchini should be no more than 1½ inches (4 cm) in diameter. Combine zucchini, onion and salt in large pot. Stir. Cover and let stand on counter 3 hours. Drain.

Add remaining ingredients. Stir often while bringing to a boil over medium-high heat. Boil, uncovered, 5 minutes. Pour into hot sterilized jars to within ¼ inch (6 mm) of top. Seal. Makes 2 pints.

Pictured on page 71.

Paré Pointer

If city air is so polluted and country air is so fresh and clean, why don't they build the cities in the country?

SPICED CRABAPPLES

Red crabapples make this a gorgeous color. So good!

Granulated sugar	6 cups	1.35 L
Water	2½ cups	575 mL
White vinegar	5 cups	1.13 L
Cinnamon sticks, broken up, about 6 inch (15 cm) length, each	2	2
Whole cloves	2 tsp.	10 mL
Crabapples with stems, blossom ends removed (small firm crabapples are best)	7 lbs.	3.17 kg

Measure sugar, water and vinegar into large pot. Stir and bring to a boil. Boil 10 minutes.

Tie cinnamon and cloves in double layer of cheesecloth. Add. Pricking skins of crabapples helps to avoid bursting while cooking. Add crabapples in single layers, 1 layer at a time. Cover and simmer until just tender, about 8 to 12 minutes. Discard spice bag. Spoon crabapples into hot sterilized jars to within 1 inch (2.5 cm) of top. Pour syrup over apples within ¼ inch (6 mm) of top. Seal. Makes 6 quarts.

China Courtesy Of: Dansk Gifts

Condiment Jars Courtesy Of: Eaton's Housewares Dept.

Glass Pitcher Courtesy Of: The Bay Housewares Dept.

Strawberry Spoon Courtesy Of: Le Gnome

Wire Basket Courtesy Of: Call The Kettle Black

LEMON BEET PICKLES

There is a difference to these pickles. Not your usual beet pickles.

Beets with 1 inch (2.5 cm) tops intact	2 lbs.	1 kg
Water to cover		
Granulated sugar	3 cups	750 mL
Slivered almonds	1 cup	250 mL
Ground ginger	1 tbsp.	15 mL
Medium lemons with peel, quartered and thinly sliced	2	2

Cook beets in water until tender. Cool in cold water until they can be handled. Peel. Dice finely into large saucepan. There should be 4 cups (900 mL).

Add sugar, almonds and ginger. Bring to a boil over medium heat, stirring frequently. Simmer slowly, uncovered, stirring occasionally, for 30 minutes.

Add lemon. Simmer 30 minutes more, stirring frequently. Pour into hot sterilized jars to within ¼ inch (6 mm) of top. Seal. Makes 3 pints.

BEET PICKLES

There are no spices added to this pickle. They have a nice tang.

Beets with 1 inch (2.5 cm) tops intact	3 lbs.	1.36 kg
Water to cover		
BRINE		
White vinegar	2 cups	500 mL
Water	2 cups	500 mL
Granulated sugar	1 cup	250 mL
Table salt	1 tsp.	5 mL

Cook beets in water in large pot until tender. Cool in cooking water until you can put your hands in comfortably. Slide off beet skins. Leave tiny beets whole. Cut larger beets into chunks. Pack into hot sterilized jars to within 1 inch (2.5 cm) of top.

Brine: While cooking water is cooling, combine vinegar, water, sugar and salt in saucepan. Heat on medium and stir often until it reaches a boil. Pour over beets in jars to within ¼ inch (6 mm) of top. Seal. Makes 3 pints.

PICKLED WATERMELON

Thick syrupy pickles with a rich color.

Water	9 cups	2.25 L
Coarse (pickling) salt	1/2 cup	125 mL
Watermelon balls (or pieces)	11 cups	2.75 L
Granulated sugar	5 cups	1.25 L
Cinnamon stick, broken up	1	1
Ground ginger	1/4 tsp.	1 mL
Lemon juice, fresh or bottled	2 tbsp.	30 mL
White vinegar	2 1/2 cups	625 mL

Stir water and salt together in large bowl. Add watermelon balls. Cover and let stand on counter overnight. Drain. Rinse and drain again.

In large pot, combine next 5 ingredients. Bring to a boil over medium-high heat, stirring occasionally. Add watermelon. Return to a boil. Reduce heat. Simmer, uncovered, for about 20 minutes. Remove cinnamon pieces. Pack fruit into hot sterilized jars to within 1 inch (2.5 cm) of top. Bring syrup to a full rolling boil on medium-high heat. Boil about 25 to 30 minutes, stirring occasionally, until it thickens. Don't boil too long or syrup will start to caramelize and change color. It will thicken a bit with a tinge of golden color. Pour syrup over fruit to within 1/4 inch (6 mm) of top. Seal. Makes 2 pints.

Pictured on page 71.

ZUCCHINI DILLS

No waiting for cucumbers to grow.

Sliced zucchini with peel, 1/8 inch (3 mm) thick	8 cups	2 L
Sliced celery	1 cup	250 mL
Sliced onion	2 cups	500 mL
Coarse (pickling) salt	1/2 cup	125 mL
Granulated sugar	2 cups	500 mL
White vinegar	2 cups	500 mL
Small garlic clove, per pint	1	1
Mustard seed, per pint	1 1/2 tsp.	7 mL
Head of dill, per pint	1	1

(continued on next page)

Place zucchini, celery, onion and salt in large pot. Stir. Let stand 2 hours. Drain well.

Heat and stir sugar and vinegar in large pot until sugar dissolves. Add zucchini mixture. Bring to a boil, stirring occasionally.

Place garlic, mustard seed and dill in each hot sterilized pint jar. Fill with vegetables to within 1 inch (2.5 cm) of top. Pour liquid to within ¼ inch (6 mm) of top. Seal. Makes 3 pints.

SWEET DILL PICKLES

A sweet pickle with a dill flavor.

Heads of dill, per quart	2	2
Garlic clove, per quart	2	2
Sliced cucumbers (fairly thick) with peel	1 qt.	1 L
BRINE		
White vinegar	3 cups	675 mL
Water	3 cups	675 mL
Granulated sugar	4½ cups	1 L
Coarse (pickling) salt	3 tbsp.	50 mL

Put 1 head of dill and garlic clove in bottom of hot sterilized 1 quart jar. Fill with cucumber to within 1 inch (2.5 cm) of top. Add second head of dill and garlic clove. Repeat to make 4 quarts.

Brine: Combine all ingredients in saucepan. Heat, stirring often, until it boils. Pour over cucumbers, filling jars to within ¼ inch (6 mm) of top. Seal. Let stand 2 to 3 weeks before eating. Makes enough brine for 4 quarts.

Pictured on page 35.

Paré Pointer

A married man kisses the misses. A bachelor misses the kisses.

PICKLED CANTALOUPE

So different to serve with a luncheon.

Large cantaloupe	3	3
Granulated sugar	3 cups	750 mL
White vinegar	2 cups	500 mL
Table salt	1 tsp.	5 mL
Cinnamon sticks, broken up	2	2
Whole cloves	1 tsp.	5 mL

Cut cantaloupe in half. Remove seeds. Scoop into balls, or peel and cut into chunks.

Combine sugar, vinegar and salt in large pot. Tie cinnamon and cloves together in double layer of cheesecloth. Add to vinegar mixture. Bring to a boil over medium-high heat, stirring often. Add cantaloupe pieces. Return to a boil. Reduce heat. Simmer, uncovered, for about 45 to 60 minutes, stirring occasionally, until cantaloupe is clear. Remove spice bag. Pack fruit into hot sterilized jars to within 1 inch (2.5 cm) of top. Fill with syrup to within 1/4 inch (6 mm) of top. Seal. Makes 3 half pints.

CHERRY PICKLES

An unusual pickle. A scene stealer!

Cherries with stems, about 2 lbs. (900 g)	8 cups	1.8 L
White vinegar	2¼ cups	500 mL
Water	2¼ cups	500 mL
Granulated sugar	6 tbsp.	100 mL
Coarse (pickling) salt	3 tbsp.	50 mL

Pack cherries into hot sterilized jars to within 1 inch (2.5 cm) of top.

Combine next 4 ingredients in saucepan. Stir. Bring to a boil on medium-high heat stirring frequently. Pour over cherries to within 1/4 inch (6 mm) of top. Seal. Let stand 2 weeks before serving. Makes 4 pints.

Pictured on cover.

PUMPKIN PICKLES

This different tasty pickle is very colorful.

Pumpkin, peeled, seeds removed, cut in 1 inch (2.5 cm) squares	4 lbs.	1.82 kg
Granulated sugar	4½ cups	1.13 L
White vinegar	2 cups	500 mL
Water	2 cups	500 mL
Thinly sliced lemon	½	½
Cinnamon stick, broken up	1	1
Whole cloves	8	8
Whole allspice	8	8

Place first 4 ingredients into large pot.

Tie lemon, cinnamon stick pieces, cloves and allspice in double layer of cheesecloth. Add to pumpkin mixture. Heat and stir until sugar dissolves. Bring to a boil. Simmer, uncovered, for about 20 minutes, stirring occasionally until pumpkin is tender. Discard spice bag. Pack pumpkin into hot sterilized jars to within 1 inch (2.5 cm) of top. Fill with syrup to within ¼ inch (6 mm) of top. Seal. Makes 4 pints.

Pictured on cover.

PICKLED GRAPES

Serve an unusual, novel pickle.

Water	1 cup	250 mL
White vinegar	1 cup	250 mL
Granulated sugar	1 cup	250 mL
Seedless grapes	1½ lbs.	680 g

Combine first 3 ingredients in saucepan. Heat and stir until sugar dissolves. Bring to a boil.

Remove stems from grapes. Fill jars with grapes. Cover with syrup. Cool. Chill for 2 or 3 days before serving. Makes 2 pints.

BUCKET PICKLES

A fantastic easy to make pickle.

Granulated sugar	4 cups	1 L
White vinegar	2 cups	500 mL
Coarse (pickling) salt	2 tbsp.	30 mL
Turmeric	1 tsp.	5 mL
Celery seed	1 tsp.	5 mL
Mustard seed	1 tsp.	5 mL
Large red pepper, seeded, cut in slices	1	1
Large green pepper, seeded, cut in slices	1	1
Large Spanish onion, cut in slices	1	1
Cucumbers with peel, thinly sliced	5	5

Measure first 6 ingredients in 4 quart (4 L) ice cream bucket. Stir.

Add red pepper, green pepper and onion. Add more or less cucumber, depending on size, to fill bucket up to level of liquid. Let stand about 2 hours. Stir. It will shrink down a bit so you may be able to add a few more cucumber slices. Cover. Store in refrigerator for up to 6 months. Makes about 2½ quarts (2.5 L).

Pictured on page 107.

FREEZER PICKLES

Good flavor and colorful. And they stay crisp!

Sliced cucumbers with peel	7 cups	1.75 L
Large onion, sliced	1	1
Thinly sliced peppers, seeded, all green or half red	1 cup	250 mL
Coarse (pickling) salt	1 tbsp.	15 mL
Celery seed	½ tsp.	2 mL
White vinegar	1 cup	250 mL
Granulated sugar	2 cups	500 mL

Combine all ingredients in bowl. Stir well. Cover. Refrigerate for 3 days. Stir every day. Pack into freezer containers, covering with brine to within 1 inch (2.5 cm) of top. Freeze. Thaw before serving. Keeps in refrigerator at least 8 weeks. Keeps in freezer at least 1 year. Makes 3 pints.

COLORFUL PICKLES

Makes a pickle from a pickle.

Sliced dill pickles, not sweet	2 cups	500 mL
Sliced pimiento	1/2 cup	125 mL
White vinegar	2/3 cup	150 mL
Water	1/3 cup	75 mL
Granulated sugar	1 cup	250 mL
Cooking oil	1 tbsp.	15 mL

Combine pickles and pimiento in bowl.

Bring next 4 ingredients to a boil on medium-high heat in saucepan, stirring occasionally. Pour over pickle mixture. Cool to room temperature. Cover and store in container in refrigerator. Let stand up to 1 week before serving. Keeps in refrigerator at least 8 weeks. Makes 1 1/2 pints.

NO-COOK PICKLES

A pickle with a crunch. You will need to make double the second time around.

Thinly sliced cucumber with peel	10 cups	2.5 L
Thinly sliced onion	2 cups	500 mL
BRINE		
Granulated sugar	2 cups	500 mL
White vinegar	1 cup	250 mL
Coarse (pickling) salt	2 tbsp.	30 mL
Celery seed	1 tsp.	5 mL
Turmeric	1 tsp.	5 mL

Combine cucumber and onion in large bowl.

Brine: Measure next 5 ingredients into saucepan. Bring to a boil on medium-high heat, stirring frequently. Boil 3 minutes. Pour over vegetables. Stir well. Cool to room temperature. Let stand 2 to 3 days in refrigerator before serving. Store, covered, in containers in refrigerator at least 8 weeks. Makes 4 pints.

HURRY MUSTARD BEANS

Make this one day and eat the next. Uses canned beans.

Granulated sugar	1¼ cups	300 mL
All-purpose flour	¼ cup	60 mL
Dry mustard powder	2 tbsp.	30 mL
Turmeric	1 tsp.	5 mL
Celery seed	1 tsp.	5 mL
White vinegar	1½ cups	375 mL
Canned cut wax beans, drained (see Note)	3 × 14 oz.	3 × 398 mL

Combine first 5 ingredients in medium size saucepan. Stir well.

Add vinegar and stir. Stir over medium heat until it boils and thickens.

Add beans. Stir lightly. Pour carefully into container. Cool to room temperature. Cover and store in refrigerator for at least 24 hours before eating. Keeps in refrigerator at least 8 weeks. Makes about 3 pints.

Note: About 4 cups (1 L) fresh beans, cooked, may be used instead of canned.

SWEET DILLS

An easy way to change a pickle you buy into a pickle you can't buy. Delicious.

Whole dill pickles, drained, cut in half lengthwise and crosswise	32 oz.	1 L
Granulated sugar	2 cups	450 mL
White vinegar	½ cup	125 mL
Celery seed	1 tbsp.	15 mL
Mustard seed	1 tbsp.	15 mL
Whole cloves	3	3

Combine all ingredients in bowl. If you would rather, pickles may be sliced. Stir. Let stand 10 minutes. Store in refrigerator, covered. Stir 2 or 3 times while in bowl. Spoon back into original bottle after 3 days. Keeps in refrigerator at least 8 weeks. Makes 32 oz. (1 L).

CHILLED ZUCCHINI PICKLES

Light colored, crunchy and tasty. Peeled zucchini lends a different look.

Peeled, thinly sliced zucchini	5 cups	1.25 L
Thinly sliced carrots	1/2 cup	125 mL
Thinly sliced onion	1/2 cup	125 mL
Sliced celery	1/2 cup	125 mL
Coarse (pickling) salt	3 tbsp.	50 mL
Water	1 cup	250 mL
Cider vinegar	1 cup	250 mL
Granulated sugar	1 cup	250 mL
Chopped pimiento	2 tbsp.	30 mL

Combine first 5 ingredients in bowl. Stir. Let stand 45 minutes. Drain. Rinse and drain again.

Place water, vinegar and sugar in saucepan. Stir and bring to a boil over medium-high heat. Pour over vegetables. Cool to room temperature.

Stir in pimiento. Fill containers. Cover and refrigerate. Let stand 2 to 3 days before eating. Keeps in refrigerator for at least 8 weeks. Makes a generous 2 1/2 pints.

GARLIC PICKLES

These taste different than you would expect. Sweet and good.

Dill pickles, not sweet, drained, sliced	32 oz.	1 L
Granulated sugar	2 1/2 cups	625 mL
Mixed pickling spice, tied in double layer of cheesecloth	2 tbsp.	30 mL
Garlic cloves	3	3

Place sliced pickles in bowl. Add sugar, pickling spice and garlic. Stir. Cover. Let stand for 1 day. Stir. Cover. Let stand for second day. On third day, stir. Discard garlic and spice bag. Spoon pickles back into bottle. Store, covered, for 2 to 3 days before eating. Keeps in refrigerator at least 4 weeks. Makes 32 oz. (1 L) jar.

Pictured on page 107.

SPEEDY BEET PICKLES

Definitely no work to these. Canned beets are marinated for a day or two and they are ready to eat. Try both kinds to determine your preference.

Canned beets, drained, juice reserved (see Note)	2 x 14 oz.	2 x 398 mL
Beet juice	1 cup	250 mL
White vinegar	1 cup	250 mL
Granulated sugar	½ cup	125 mL
Table salt	½ tsp.	2 mL

Cut larger beets. Leave tiny ones whole. Place in jar.

Combine beet juice, vinegar, sugar and salt in container. Stir until sugar dissolves. Pour over beets. Cover. Chill for 1 or 2 days before serving. Keeps in refrigerator for at least 4 weeks. Makes 1 quart.

SPICED PICKLED BEETS: Add ½ cup (125 mL) sugar and 1 tbsp. (15 mL) mixed pickling spice that you have tied in a double layer of cheesecloth. Boil over medium heat 5 minutes. Discard spice bag. Pour brine over beets. Chill for 1 or 2 days before serving. Keeps in refrigerator at least 4 weeks.

Note: Fresh cooked beets, about 3½ cups (800 mL) may be used instead of canned.

PICKLED PEPPERED EGGS

Not only eggs but colored peppers also. Great entertaining idea. Small eggs will make more servings.

Large hard-boiled eggs, shelled	12	12
Yellow pepper, seeded and cut in strips	1	1
Red pepper, seeded and cut in strips	1	1
Green pepper, seeded and cut in strips	1	1
Large onion, cut in rings	1	1
BRINE		
White vinegar	2 cups	500 mL
Water	1 cup	250 mL
Granulated sugar	¼ cup	60 mL
Whole cloves, tied in double layer of cheesecloth	8-10	8-10
Table salt	1 tsp.	5 mL

(continued on next page)

Arrange eggs a few at a time in 2 quart jar. Place colored peppers and onions around them, mixing them for color as you fill jar.

Brine: In saucepan, bring all 5 ingredients to a boil over medium-high heat, stirring often. Boil 5 minutes. Discard spice bag. Pour over egg mixture. Brine must cover completely. Cover and store in refrigerator 4 days or more before eating. Keeps in refrigerator at least 6 months. Makes 2 quarts.

Pictured on page 107.

SWEET PICKLED EGGS

Lightly touched with pickling spice. Keeps in refrigerator for at least six months.

Large hard-boiled eggs, shelled	12	12
Cold water to cover		
Large onion, sliced in rings	1	1
BRINE		
White vinegar	2 cups	500 mL
Water	2 cups	500 mL
Granulated sugar	1/2 cup	125 mL
Table salt	1 tsp.	5 mL
Mixed pickling spice, tied in double layer of cheesecloth	1 tbsp.	15 mL

Cover eggs with water in large saucepan. Cover. Bring to a boil over medium-high heat. Boil gently for 10 minutes. Drain. Run cold water over eggs until they are cold. Shell.

Layer whole eggs and onion rings in 2 quart jar to within 1 inch (2.5 cm) of top.

Brine: Combine vinegar, water, sugar and salt in saucepan. Stir over medium heat until sugar dissolves. Bring to a boil. Remove from heat.

Add pickling spice. Swish bag around for 30 seconds. Remove bag. Pour brine over eggs to fill jars to within 1/4 inch (6 mm) of top. Seal. Let stand 1 to 2 weeks in refrigerator before serving. Serve chilled. Use small eggs for more servings. Makes 2 quarts.

BEET AND CABBAGE PICKLE

An old hometown recipe. Just the right amount of horseradish. A real beef go-with.

Chopped, cooked fresh beets (see Note)	1 cup	250 mL
Chopped cabbage, packed	1 cup	250 mL
Granulated sugar	½ cup	125 mL
Bottled horseradish	¼ cup	60 mL
Table salt	¾ tsp	4 mL
Pepper	¼ tsp.	1 mL
White vinegar	1 tbsp.	15 mL

Combine all ingredients in bowl. Stir well. More vinegar may be added now or after it has marinated. Go by taste. Turn into jar. Cover and let stand in refrigerator for 2 days before serving. Serve with hot or cold beef. Keeps for at least 4 weeks. Makes about 1 pint.

Note: Canned beets, 14 oz. (398 mL), may also be used.

CHERRY PIE FILLING

Tastes like a fresh cherry pie.

Cherries, pitted	8 cups	2 L
Water	2 cups	500 mL
Granulated sugar	2 cups	500 mL
Minute tapioca	6 tbsp.	100 mL
Almond flavoring	½ tsp.	2 mL

Place all 5 ingredients in large pot. Stir as you bring to a boil over medium-high heat. Pack fruit into hot sterilized quart jars to within 1 inch (2.5 cm) of top. Fill with juice to within ½ inch (12 mm) of top. Secure lids. Process in hot water bath for 25 minutes. Makes 2 quarts, enough for two 9 inch (22 cm) pies.

Make your own mincemeat this easy way. Serve warm mincemeat pie with ice cream or slices of medium Cheddar cheese.

Ground beef suet, about 2 cups (500 mL)	8 oz.	250 g
Brown sugar, packed	3 cups	750 mL
Tart apples, peeled, cored and chopped	5 cups	1.25 L
Raisins	2 cups	500 mL
Currants	2 cups	500 mL
Cut mixed peel, about 1½ cups (350 mL)	8 oz.	250 g
White vinegar	½ cup	125 mL
Ground cinnamon	1 tsp.	5 mL
Nutmeg	1 tsp.	5 mL
Ground cloves	¼ tsp.	1 mL
Table salt	½ tsp.	2 mL
Raisins	1 cup	250 mL
Currants	1 cup	250 mL

In large container, measure first 11 ingredients. Stir together. Put this mixture through grinder or use food processor.

Mix in remaining raisins and currants. They can all be ground if you like. With some whole fruit it resembles the commercial variety. Cover. Refrigerate and allow to stand 2 to 3 days to mellow. This keeps for over a year in refrigerator. It may also be frozen or, if you prefer, you can bring to a boil and seal in hot sterilized jars. Makes 4 pints.

MINCEMEAT PIE: For a 9 inch (22 cm) pie, use 2 cups (450 mL) mincemeat, ¾ cup (175 mL) apple sauce and 1½ tbsp. (25 mL) minute tapioca. Bake on bottom shelf of 400°F (200°C) oven about 30 to 35 minutes, until browned.

Paré Pointer

When someone calls you a dumb flower, he really means you're a bloomin' idiot.

PEAR MINCEMEAT

Be sure to try this not-so-common mincemeat in pear season. Extra good.

Granulated sugar	6 cups	1.5 L
Ground cinnamon	1 tsp.	5 mL
Ground allspice	1 tsp.	5 mL
Ground cloves	1 tsp.	5 mL
Table salt	1 tsp.	5 mL
Pears, peeled and cored	8 lbs.	3.63 kg
Orange with rind, quartered and seeded	1	1
Lemon with rind, quartered and seeded	1	1
Tart apple, peeled and cored	1	1
Grape juice (purple)	1 cup	250 mL
Cider vinegar	1 cup	250 mL
Raisins	3 cups	750 mL
Currants	3⅓ cups	825 mL

Measure first 5 ingredients into large pot. Stir.

Grind next 4 ingredients into same pot. Stir well.

Add remaining ingredients. Bring to a boil over medium heat, stirring often. Simmer, uncovered, until thick. Spoon into hot sterilized jars to within ¼ inch (6 mm) of top. Seal. This also freezes well. If stored in containers in refrigerator, it keeps at least 1 year. Makes 6 pints.

PEAR MINCEMEAT PIE: To make a 9 inch (22 cm) pie from this recipe, use 2 cups (500 mL) mincemeat, ¾ cup (175 mL) apple sauce and 1½ tbsp. (25 mL) minute tapioca. Bake on bottom shelf of 400°F (200°C) oven about 30 to 35 minutes, until browned.

Paré Pointer

There are two cures for alimony. Stay married or stay single.

GREEN TOMATO MINCEMEAT

Use your extra green tomatoes for this excellent filling. Keeps for months in the refrigerator. It also freezes well.

Finely chopped green tomatoes, about 2½ lbs. (1.15 kg)	10 cups	2.25 L
Water to cover		
Apples, peeled, cored and chopped	5 cups	1.25 L
Ground suet	2 cups	500 mL
Raisins	2 cups	500 mL
Currants	1 cup	250 mL
Cut mixed peel	1 cup	250 mL
Granulated sugar	3 cups	700 mL
Brown sugar, packed	3 cups	700 mL
Ground cinnamon	1 tbsp.	15 mL
Nutmeg	1 tbsp.	15 mL
Ground cloves	1 tsp.	5 mL
Ground allspice	1 tsp.	5 mL
Table salt	1 tsp.	5 mL
White vinegar	½ cup	125 mL

Combine tomatoes and water in large pot. Bring to a boil, stirring often. Boil gently for 30 minutes. Drain.

Add next 7 ingredients. Bring to a boil. Boil gently until thick, about 2 hours. Stir frequently to prevent scorching.

Stir in remaining 6 ingredients. Pour into hot sterilized jars to within ¼ inch (6 mm) of top. Seal. This can also be cooled and frozen or stored for months in refrigerator. Makes about 5 pints.

GREEN TOMATO MINCEMEAT PIE: For a 9 inch (22 cm) pie, use 2 cups (500 mL) mincemeat, ¾ cup (175 mL) applesauce and 1½ tbsp. (25 mL) minute tapioca. Bake on bottom shelf of 400°F (200°C) oven about 30 to 35 minutes, until browned.

Paré Pointer

As a minister rehearses his sermon you could say he practices what he preaches.

APPLE PIE FILLING

This is the answer if your freezer is full. Keeps on the shelf until needed.

Peeled, cored, cut up apples	**5 cups**	**1.25 L**
Granulated sugar	**1 cup**	**250 mL**
Minute tapioca	**2 tbsp.**	**30 mL**
Ground cinnamon	**½ tsp.**	**2 mL**
Lemon juice, fresh or bottled (optional)	**1 tsp.**	**5 mL**

Combine apples and sugar in large pot. Stir. Let stand until juice starts to be released. Stir as you bring it to a boil over medium-high heat. Boil hard for 1 minute.

Mix in tapioca, cinnamon and lemon juice. Boil hard for 1 minute more. Pack into hot sterilized quart jars to within ½ inch (12 mm) of top. Secure lids. Process in hot water bath for 20 minutes. Repeat for as many jars as you like. Makes 1 quart, enough for one 9 inch (22 cm) pie.

Pictured on page 71.

1. Bucket Pickles page 96
2. Tri-Veg Pickles page 73
3. Pickled Snow Peas page 76
4. Sweet Mustard Pickles page 74
5. Pickled Peppered Eggs page 100
6. Beet Relish page 127
7. Pickled Garlic page 65
8. Apple Relish page 123
9. Paw Paw Pickles page 65
10. Garlic Pickles page 99
11. Peach Pickles page 80
12. Chow Chow Maritime page 69
13. Fresh Crabapples
14. Pickled Onions page 75
15. Million Dollar Relish page 129
16. Pickled Beets page 66
17. Curry Pickles page 82

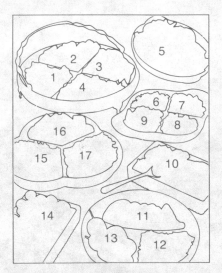

Cloverleaf Relish Dish Courtesy Of: Pickle/Relish Dishes Courtesy Of:
Birks Jewellers   Eaton's China Dept.

It is not considered safe to preserve meats and vegetables by any other method than pressure canning. It is a chance not worth taking. Use washed, young, tender vegetables, the fresher the better when canning vegetables. When canning meats, use good quality. Pressure pounds and times are included in each recipe. However, be sure to check with your pressure cooker-canner instructions.

VEGETABLES

Lacking freezer space? The answer is to preserve your own vegetables.

ASPARAGUS: Break off tough ends of fresh asparagus. Cut lengths to fit jars. Pack, stem ends down, leaving 1 inch (2.5 cm) headroom. If you prefer, stalks may be cut in short lengths and packed loosely. Add ½ tsp. (2 mL) coarse (pickling) salt per pint, 1 tsp. (5 mL) per quart. Fill with boiling water to within 1 inch (2.5 cm) of top. Secure lids. Pressure cook at 10 pounds pressure for 30 minutes for pints, 35 minutes for quarts.

BEANS: Cut off ends from newly ripened green or wax beans. Cut into 1 inch (2.5 cm) lengths, leave them whole or slice lengthwise. Pack loosely in jars leaving 1 inch (2.5 cm) headroom. Add ½ tsp. (2 mL) coarse (pickling) salt per pint, 1 tsp. (5 mL) per quart. Fill with boiling water to within 1 inch (2.5 cm) of top. Secure lids. Pressure cook at 10 pounds pressure for 20 minutes for pints, 25 minutes for quarts.

BEETS: In large pot cover beets, with 2 inch (5 cm) stem ends intact, with water. Cook for 20 to 25 minutes so that skins will remove easily under cold water. Pack hot beets into jars leaving 1 inch (2.5 cm) headroom. Add ½ tsp. (2 mL) coarse (pickling) salt to each pint, 1 tsp. (5 mL) for each quart. Fill with boiling water to within 1 inch (2.5 cm) of top. Secure lids. Pressure cook at 10 pounds pressure for 30 minutes for pints, 35 minutes for quarts.

(continued on next page)

CARROTS: Scrub tender young carrots with a plastic pot scraper. Pack into jars leaving 1 inch (2.5 cm) headroom. Add ½ tsp. (2 mL) coarse (pickling) salt to each pint, 1 tsp. (5 mL), to each quart. Fill with boiling water to within 1 inch (2.5 cm) of top. Secure lids. Pressure cook at 10 pounds pressure for 30 minutes for pints, 35 minutes for quarts.

CORN, CREAM-STYLE: Using sharp knife, cut down side of freshly ripened cob, cutting through middle of kernels. Using blunt edge of knife or table knife, scrape down sides of cobs to get the "cream". Pack loosely in pint jars, leaving 1 inch (2.5 cm) headroom. Add ½ tsp. (2 mL) each, of coarse (pickling) salt, granulated sugar and lemon juice to each pint. Fill with boiling water to within 1 inch (2.5 cm) of top. Secure lids. Pressure cook at 10 pounds pressure for 85 minutes for pints.

CORN KERNELS: Cut kernels from freshly ripened cobs. Cut fairly close to cob, but not so close that you get the hulls. Pack lightly in pint jars, leaving 1 inch (2.5 cm) headroom. Add ½ tsp. (2 mL) coarse (pickling) salt to each pint. Fill with boiling water to within 1 inch (2.5 cm) of top. Secure lids. Pressure cook at 10 pounds pressure for 55 minutes for pints, 85 minutes for quarts.

PEAS: Fill jars with tender young peas, leaving 1 inch (2.5 cm) headroom. Add ½ tsp. (2 mL) each of coarse (pickling) salt and granulated sugar to each pint, 1 tsp. (5 mL) each of coarse (pickling) salt and sugar to each quart. Fill with boiling water to within 1 inch (2.5 cm) of top. Secure lids. Pressure cook at 10 pounds pressure for 40 minutes for pints, 45 minutes for quarts.

Paré Pointer

If you have a calculator and some rubber bands, you have a computer that makes snap decisions.

Just heat and serve. Great for camping.

Finely minced onion	**1 cup**	**250 mL**
Dry bread crumbs	**1 cup**	**250 mL**
Water	**1 cup**	**250 mL**
Beef bouillon powder	**2 tsp.**	**10 mL**
Table salt	**1 tsp.**	**5 mL**
Pepper	**½ tsp.**	**2 mL**
Garlic powder	**¼ tsp.**	**1 mL**
Lean ground beef	**2¼ lbs.**	**1 kg**
Boiling water	**6 cups**	**1.5 L**
Beef bouillon powder	**2 tbsp.**	**30 mL**

Combine first 7 ingredients in bowl. Stir together well.

Add ground beef. Mix. Shape into 18 patties. Brown both sides in greased frying pan. Pack into hot sterilized jars without breaking patties, leaving 1 inch (2.5 cm) space at top.

Stir boiling water and second amount of bouillon powder together. Pour over meat patties leaving 1 inch (2.5 cm) space at top. Secure lids. Process in pressure canner at 10 pounds pressure, 75 minutes for pints, 90 minutes for quarts. Makes 3 quarts.

Pictured on page 35.

MEATBALLS: Shape meat mixture into meatballs instead of patties.

A kettle is a water 'otter.

STEWED TOMATOES

Similar to store-bought.

Ripe tomatoes	**6 lbs.**	**2.75 kg**
Finely chopped onion	**¾ cup**	**175 mL**
Finely chopped celery	**¾ cup**	**175 mL**
Finely chopped green pepper	**¼ cup**	**50 mL**
Coarse (pickling) salt	**2 tsp.**	**10 mL**
Granulated sugar	**2 tsp.**	**10 mL**

Dip tomatoes in boiling water for about 1 minute. Peel. Coarsely chop tomatoes. Put into large pot.

Add remaining ingredients. Bring to a boil, stirring often, on medium-high heat. Fill jars to within 1 inch (2.5 cm) of top. Secure lids. Process in pressure cooker at 10 pounds pressure for 30 minutes, 35 minutes for quarts. When finished, jars will be watery at the bottom but will be fine when stirred. Makes 6 pints.

PORK AND BEANS

A camper's special.

Dried white beans	**3 lbs.**	**1.36 kg**
Water to cover well		
Ham, diced	**1½ lbs.**	**680 g**
Onion flakes	**½ cup**	**125 mL**
Ketchup	**2 cups**	**450 mL**
Molasses	**½ cup**	**125 mL**
Coarse (pickling) salt	**2 tsp.**	**10 mL**

Soak beans in lots of water overnight in large heavy saucepan. Drain next morning. Cover with water again. Bring to a boil, stirring occasionally, on medium heat. Cover. Cook about 1 hour until tender but not too soft. Bite into a bean to check if cooked. Stir often while cooking.

Add remaining ingredients. Stir. Return to a boil. Pour into jars to within 1 inch (2.5 cm) of top. Secure lids. Process in pressure canner at 10 pounds pressure for 80 minutes per pint, 100 minutes per quart. To serve, add a bit of water to thin slightly. Makes 10 pints or 5 quarts.

Pictured on page 71.

A whole meal in a jar.

Margarine (butter browns too fast)	1 tbsp.	15 mL
Boneless beef round steak	2¼ lbs.	1 kg.
Cubed onion	3 cups	750 mL
Cubed potatoes	3 cups	750 mL
Cubed carrots	3 cups	750 mL
Cubed turnip	1½ cups	375 mL
Peas	1 cup	250 mL
Sliced celery	1 cup	250 mL
Coarse (pickling) salt, per quart	1 tsp.	5 mL
Water	1½ cups	375 mL
Hot water	1 cup	250 mL
Beef bouillon powder	1 tsp.	5 mL

Heat margarine in frying pan. Brown meat well on both sides, as brown as possible without tasting burned. Cut into bite size cubes and place in large bowl.

Add next 6 vegetables. Toss to distribute pieces evenly. Pack into quart sealers leaving 1 inch (2.5 cm) headroom.

Add 1 tsp. (5 mL) salt per quart.

Pour first amount of water into frying pan. Stir to loosen any brown bits. Divide among jars.

Mix remaining water and bouillon powder, making more as needed using same proportion. Fill jars to 1 inch (2.5 cm) from top. Secure lids. Pressure cook at 10 pounds pressure for 90 minutes for quarts, 75 minutes for pints. Makes 5 quarts.

Paré Pointer

If you are a first-time car owner, you will find the first thing your car runs into is money.

TOMATO SOUP

A smooth flavorful soup. Add an equal amount of water to serve.

Ripe tomatoes, quartered	8 lbs.	3.62 kg
Sliced celery	2 cups	500 mL
Medium onion, chopped	1	1
Large green pepper, seeded and chopped	1	1
Parsley sprigs	6	6
Whole cloves	6	6
Bay leaves	6	6
Butter or margarine	4 tbsp.	60 mL
All-purpose flour	¾ cup	175 mL
Table salt	2½ tbsp.	35 mL

Place first 4 ingredients in large pot. Bring to a boil.

Tie parsley, cloves and bay leaves in double layer of cheesecloth. Add to pot. Cook, uncovered, until tender stirring occasionally. Remove spice bag. Press through food mill or sieve into large saucepan.

Melt butter in small saucepan. Stir in flour and salt. Add a bit of purée to mix smooth. In large saucepan bring purée to a boil. Stir in flour mixture until it boils and thickens. Pour into jars to within 1 inch (2.5 cm) of top. Secure lids. Process in pressure cooker at 10 pounds pressure, 25 minutes for pints, 30 minutes for quarts. Makes 4 pints.

CANNED SALMON

Wonderful on a hot day served with a salad.

Fresh salmon, with or without bones, per pint	8 oz.	250 g
Coarse (pickling) salt, per pint	½ tsp.	2 mL
Cooking oil, per pint	1 tsp.	5 mL

Cut salmon into pieces and pack in pint jars to within 1 inch (2.5 cm) of top. Add salt and cooking oil. Secure lids. Process in pressure cooker at 10 pounds pressure for 100 minutes. Makes as much as you like depending on how much salmon you have.

Pictured on page 17.

CANNED CHICKEN

Multiply this by as many quarts as you want. Very good and very handy.

Fresh chicken pieces, use meaty parts only, with skin intact, per quart	1³/₄ **lbs.**	**800 g**
Coarse (pickling) salt, per quart	**1 tsp.**	**5 mL**

Pack chicken into quart jar to within 1 inch (2.5 cm) of top. Spoon salt over top. Secure lids. Cook in pressure cooker at 10 pounds pressure for 75 minutes for quarts, 65 minutes for pints. Make as many jars as you like.

FISH CATCH

With or without bone, this is great to have on hand. Bones soften when processed.

Fresh fish, your own catch or store-bought, per pint	**8 oz.**	**250 g**
Ketchup, per pint	**2 tbsp.**	**30 mL**
White vinegar, per pint	1½ **tsp.**	**7 mL**
Cooking oil, per pint	**2 tsp.**	**10 mL**
Coarse (pickling) salt, per pint	½ **tsp.**	**2 mL**

Cut fish with bones, into pieces. Pack into pint jars leaving 1 inch (2.5 cm) headroom.

Mix ketchup, vinegar, cooking oil and salt together. Place over top of fish. Repeat for more jars. Secure lids. Pressure cook at 10 pounds pressure for 100 minutes. Let stand 4 to 6 weeks before serving. Makes as much as you like.

Paré Pointer

The jungle hunters were surprised to find lions were religious when they heard them say "Let us prey."

BEEFY SOUP

No hidden ingredients when you make this good soup yourself.

Beef bouillon cubes	3 × ⅕ oz.	3 × 6 g
Boiling water	2 cups	500 mL
Bay leaves	2	2
Table salt	1½ tsp.	7 mL
Pepper	½ tsp.	2 mL
Beef, diced	1 lb.	454 g
Ripe medium tomatoes, peeled and coarsely chopped	6	6
Chopped potato	1 cup	250 mL
Chopped cabbage	1 cup	250 mL
Chopped onion	1 cup	250 mL
Chopped celery	1 cup	250 mL
Chopped carrot	1 cup	250 mL
Granulated sugar	1 tsp.	5 mL
Dried basil	¼ tsp.	1 mL

Combine bouillon cubes and water in large pot. Stir until cubes dissolve.

Add bay leaves, salt, pepper, beef and tomatoes. Cover. Bring to a boil, stirring often. Allow to simmer for 1 hour. If it gets almost dry, add more water.

Add remaining ingredients. Stir. Continue to simmer for 20 minutes. Divide solids among 5 pint jars. Divide liquid over top. Add boiling water if needed to fill jars to 1 inch (2.5 cm) from top. Secure lids. Process in pressure canner at 10 pounds pressure for 75 minutes for pints, 90 minutes for quarts. To serve, add equal amount of water and heat. Add salt to taste. Makes 5 pints.

Pictured on page 17.

Paré Pointer

If you allow your sheep to study karate, you're apt to get a lamb chop.

CANNED BEEF

A jiffy meal to have in the storage room. Can be eaten cold or warm with the juices thickened.

Boneless beef, such as stewing beef	8¼ lbs.	3.75 kg
Coarse (pickling) salt, per pint	½ tsp.	2 mL

Pack meat into 8 pint jars to within 1 inch (2.5 cm) of top. Put ½ tsp. (2 mL) salt over top of meat in each jar. Secure lids. Pressure cook at 10 pounds pressure for 75 minutes for pints, 90 minutes for quarts. To can beef in quarts, use 1 tsp. (5 mL) salt per jar. Makes 8 pints or 4 quarts.

CANNED PORK: Use boneless pork instead of beef.

ZUCCHINI RELISH

An economical relish, especially if you grow your own zucchini.

Ground zucchini with peel	5 cups	1.25 L
Ground onion	2 cups	500 mL
Coarse (pickling) salt	2½ tbsp.	40 mL
Small green pepper, seeded and ground	1	1
Small red pepper, seeded and ground	1	1
White vinegar	1¼ cups	300 mL
Granulated sugar	2½ cups	625 mL
Celery seed	1 tbsp.	15 mL
Cornstarch	2 tsp.	10 mL
Dry mustard powder	1½ tsp.	7 mL
Turmeric	1½ tsp.	7 mL
Nutmeg	1½ tsp.	7 mL
Pepper	¼ tsp.	1 mL

Combine zucchini, onion and salt in large bowl. Cover and let stand overnight on counter. Drain. Rinse in cold water. Drain. Turn into large pot.

Add remaining ingredients. Heat on medium-high, stirring often, until it boils. Boil, uncovered, for 30 minutes, stirring occasionally. Pour into hot sterilized jars to within ¼ inch (6 mm) of top. Seal. Makes 5 to 6 half pint jars.

THOUSAND ISLAND RELISH

Good on anything.

Large cucumbers with peel, quartered, seeds removed	14	14
Medium onions	10	10
Red peppers, seeded	2	2
Green peppers, seeded	2	2
Coarse (pickling) salt	1/3 cup	75 mL
SAUCE		
Granulated sugar	8 cups	1.8 L
Dry mustard powder	5 tbsp.	75 mL
Ground ginger	2 tbsp.	30 mL
Turmeric	1 tbsp.	15 mL
Water	1 cup	250 mL
White vinegar	4 cups	900 mL
Cornstarch	1/3 cup	75 mL
Water	1/4 cup	60 mL

Grind first 4 ingredients into large bowl. Add salt. Cover and let stand overnight on counter. Drain next morning.

Sauce: Stir first 4 ingredients well in large heavy pot. Mix in water. Add vinegar. Stir well. Add drained vegetables. Heat on medium-high, stirring often until it comes to a boil. Boil 10 minutes, stirring occasionally.

Mix cornstarch and water in small bowl. Stir into boiling mixture. Return to a boil. Boil 1 minute, continuing to stir until thickened. Pour into hot sterilized jars to within 1/4 inch (6 mm) of top. Seal. Makes 8 1/2 pints.

Paré Pointer

Mechanics shouldn't go out in thunderstorms for fear of greased lightning.

A large recipe for family and friends. Good with hot dogs and other meat too.

VEGETABLES

Onions	5 lbs.	2.5 kg
Cucumbers with peel, seeds removed	5 lbs.	2.5 kg
Celery hearts	2	2
Green peppers, seeds removed	3	3
Red peppers, seeds removed	3	3
Large cauliflower head	1	1
Coarse (pickling) salt	¾ cup	175 mL

SAUCE

Granulated sugar	6 cups	1.5 L
All-purpose flour	2 cups	500 mL
Turmeric	1 tbsp.	15 mL
White vinegar	5 cups	1.25 L
Water	3½ cups	875 mL

Vegetables: Wash and cut vegetables into chunks. Put through food grinder.

Sprinkle salt over vegetables in large bowl. Add enough water just to cover. Cover and let stand overnight on counter. Next morning, drain very well. Press down on vegetables to squeeze out juice.

Sauce: Put all ingredients into large pot. Whisk over medium heat until it boils. Simmer and stir for 2 to 3 minutes. Add vegetables. Stir over medium heat until boiling. Remove from heat. Pour into hot sterilized jars to within ¼ inch (6 mm) of top. Seal. Makes 13 pints.

Pictured on page 35.

MUSTARD CUCUMBER RELISH

A great companion for cook-outs, whether hot dogs, ham steaks or hamburgers.

Large cucumber with peel	1	1
Small chopped cucumbers, peeled	12	12
Finely chopped onion	8 cups	1 L
Celery head, finely chopped	1	1
Red peppers, seeded and finely chopped	3	3
Coarse (pickling) salt	½ cup	125 mL
Warm water to cover		
Large cauliflower	1	1
Water	3 cups	675 mL
Granulated sugar	8 cups	2 L
White vinegar	4 cups	1 L
Mustard seed	2 tbsp.	30 mL
Celery seed	2 tbsp.	30 mL
SAUCE		
Dry mustard powder	¼ cup	60 mL
All-purpose flour	1 cup	250 mL
Turmeric	1 tbsp.	15 mL
White vinegar	1½ cups	375 mL

Use food processor or coarse blade on grinder for chopping. Combine first 6 ingredients in large pot. Cover with first amount of water. Stir. Cover and let stand on counter overnight. Drain.

Break cauliflower into florets. Cut stems up fairly fine. Put into saucepan along with second amount of water. Cover. Cook tender-crisp. Do not overcook. Drain. Add other vegetables.

Add next 4 ingredients to vegetables. Heat on medium, stirring occasionally, until it boils. Boil for 5 minutes, stirring often so it doesn't burn.

Sauce: Stir mustard, flour and turmeric together in small bowl. Mix in vinegar until smooth. Stir into boiling vegetables. Simmer for 10 minutes, stirring often. Pour into hot sterilized jars to within ¼ inch (6 mm) from top. Seal. Makes 9½ pints.

Looks fantastic with red dots throughout the yellow corn.

Fresh sweet corn cobs	9	9
Green pepper, seeded and finely chopped	1	1
Red pepper, seeded and finely chopped	1	1
Medium onion, finely chopped	1	1
Finely chopped celery	½ cup	125 mL
Table salt	½ tsp.	2 mL
Granulated sugar	2¼ cups	550 mL
White vinegar	2¼ cups	550 mL
Celery seed	½ tsp.	2 mL
Dry mustard powder	1 tsp.	5 mL
Cornstarch	1 tbsp.	15 mL
Turmeric	½ tsp.	2 mL
Water	2 tbsp.	30 mL

Cut corn (don't scrape) from cobs. You should have 4 cups (1 L). Turn into large pot.

Add next 8 ingredients. Stir. Bring to a boil over medium-high heat, stirring often. Reduce heat. Simmer, uncovered, for 30 minutes, stirring occasionally

Mix last 4 ingredients in small dish. Stir into simmering vegetables. Stir as it returns to a low boil and thickens. Pour into hot sterilized jars to within ¼ inch (6 mm) of top. Seal. Makes 6 half pints.

Pictured on page 71.

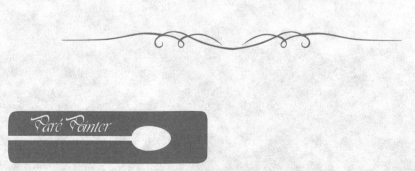

Paré Pointer

The easiest project to finish ahead of time is a two-week diet.

SWISS CHARD RELISH

A great use for this vegetable. Economy plus.

Swiss chard, white stalks only, diced	10 cups	2.25 L
Coarse (pickling) salt	¼ cup	60 mL
Medium onions, diced	2	2
White vinegar	2 cups	500 mL
Granulated sugar	2 cups	500 mL
Celery seed	1½ tsp.	7 mL
Mustard seed	½ tsp.	2 mL
SAUCE		
Cornstarch	¼ cup	60 mL
Mustard powder	1 tsp.	5 mL
Turmeric	½ tsp.	2 mL
Curry powder	½ tsp.	2 mL
Water	¼ cup	60 mL

Place chard in large pot. Sprinkle with salt. Let stand 2 hours.

Stir in onion. Let stand ½ hour. Drain well.

Add vinegar, sugar, celery seed and mustard seed. Bring to a boil, stirring often. Cook for about 30 minutes or so, stirring occasionally, until tender.

Sauce: In small bowl mix cornstarch, mustard powder, turmeric and curry powder.

Stir in water. Mix smooth. Stir into boiling chard mixture. Boil for 10 minutes more, stirring often. Fill hot sterilized jars to within ¼ inch (6 mm) of top. Seal. Makes 7 half pints.

Paré Pointer

If you have an elastic trumpet, you could play in a rubber band.

Spicy hot. Excellent with pork or any meat.

Tart apples, peeled, cored and sliced	**2 lbs.**	**1 kg**
Granulated sugar	**2 cups**	**500 mL**
Water	**½ cup**	**125 mL**
Ground ginger	**1 tbsp.**	**15 mL**
Ground almonds	**3½ oz.**	**100 g**
Raisins	**1½ cups**	**375 mL**
Mustard seed	**4 tsp.**	**20 mL**
Cayenne pepper, scant measure	**1 tbsp.**	**15 mL**
Granulated sugar	**1 cup**	**250 mL**
White vinegar	**1 cup**	**250 mL**
Table salt	**1 tbsp.**	**15 mL**

Combine first 4 ingredients in large saucepan. Bring to a boil over medium heat. Cook, uncovered, until apples are soft.

Add almonds, raisins, mustard seed and cayenne. Stir. Cook, uncovered, stirring often, until consistency of jam.

In another saucepan, combine second amount of sugar, vinegar and salt. Stir. Boil, uncovered, over medium heat until it is reduced in quantity and thickens a bit. Stir often while thickening. Watch closely so it doesn't brown. Add to apples. Stir well. Pour into hot sterilized jars to within ¼ inch (6 mm) of top. Seal. Makes 2 pints plus a small jar.

Pictured on page 107.

Paré Pointer

Cruel farmers always pull corn by the ears.

CARROT RELISH

A tangy, orange-flecked relish. Ready for hot dogs.

Ground carrots, lightly packed	2 cups	500 mL
Ground cucumber with peel (about 2½ lbs., 1.14 kg)	4 cups	1 L
Ground onion	1½ cups	1.5 L
Coarse (pickling) salt	2 tbsp.	30 mL
Granulated sugar	2¼ cups	550 mL
White vinegar	1½ cups	375 mL
Celery seed	1½ tsp.	7 mL
Mustard seed	1½ tsp.	7 mL

Put vegetables into large pot. Mix in salt. Cover and let stand on counter 3 hours. Drain thoroughly.

Add sugar, vinegar, celery seed and mustard seed. Heat on medium, stirring until sugar dissolves. Cook, uncovered, for 20 minutes, stirring occasionally. Stir more often near end of cooking time. Pour into hot sterilized jars to within ¼ inch (6 mm) of top. Seal. Makes 5 half pints.

1. Apple Chutney page 22
2. Curried Fruit page 33
3. Snap Beans page 140
4. Mustard Beans page 81
5. Pear Chutney page 24
6. Banana Chutney page 20
7. Mint Jelly page 42

PRAIRIE RELISH

This dark smooth relish goes great with any kind of meat.

Ripe tomatoes, sliced	12	12
Medium onions, sliced	5	5
Raisins	3 cups	750 mL
Table salt	1 tbsp.	15 mL
Brown sugar, packed	3 cups	750 mL
Dry mustard powder	2 tbsp.	30 mL
White vinegar	3 cups	750 mL
Whole cloves, tied in double layer of cheesecloth	5	5

Put first 4 ingredients into large pot. Bring to a boil over medium heat. Cover and simmer 2 hours, stirring 2 or 3 times. Press through food mill or sieve. Return purée to pot.

Add remaining ingredients. Bring to a boil over medium heat. Simmer, uncovered, stirring frequently, for 15 minutes. Discard spice bag. Pour into hot sterilized jars to within ¼ inch (6 mm) of top. Seal. Makes 4 pints.

BEET RELISH

Pretty color. Serve with cold or hot meats.

Cooked, peeled and diced or ground beets	4 cups	1 L
Grated cabbage	4 cups	1 L
Chopped onion	1 cup	250 mL
Prepared horseradish	1 tbsp.	15 mL
White vinegar	2 cups	500 mL
Granulated sugar	1½ cups	375 mL
Coarse (pickling) salt	1 tbsp.	15 mL
Pepper	½ tsp.	2 mL

Combine all ingredients in large pot. Bring to a boil, stirring often. Simmer for 3 minutes. Fill hot sterilized jars to within ¼ inch (6 mm) of top. Seal. Makes 8 half pints.

Pictured on page 107.

CAULI-CUKE RELISH

This bright colored relish can be made any time of year.

Medium cucumbers, peeled, cut and seeded	6	6
Large onions, cut up	4	4
Cauliflower head, cut up	1	1
Coarse (pickling) salt	3 tbsp.	50 mL
SAUCE		
Granulated sugar	3 cups	750 mL
All-purpose flour	½ cup	125 mL
Dry mustard powder	3 tbsp.	50 mL
Turmeric	1 tsp.	5 mL
Ground ginger	1 tsp.	5 mL
Pepper	¼ tsp.	1 mL
Hot water	2 cups	500 mL
White vinegar	2 cups	500 mL
Mixed pickling spice, tied in double layer of cheesecloth	3 tbsp.	50 mL

Put cucumbers, onions and cauliflower through food grinder. Mix in salt. Cover and let stand on counter 3 hours. Drain.

Sauce: Stir first 6 ingredients together in large saucepan.

Mix in hot water. Add vinegar and spice bag. Heat on medium-high, stirring often, until it comes to a boil. Boil 10 minutes, stirring occasionally. Discard spice bag. Add vegetables to sauce. Stir. Pour into hot sterilized jars to within ¼ inch (6 mm) of top. Seal. Makes 5 pints.

RHUBARB RELISH

A good condiment. Try with hot dogs, hamburgers and other meats.

Chopped rhubarb	5 cups	1.25 L
Chopped onion	5 cups	1.25 L
Cider vinegar	2½ cups	625 mL
Brown sugar, packed	6 cups	1.5 L
Table salt	1 tbsp.	15 mL
Pepper	1 tsp.	5 mL
Ground cinnamon	1 tsp.	5 mL
Ground cloves	1 tsp.	5 mL

(continued on next page)

Put rhubarb, onion and vinegar into large saucepan. Bring to a boil over medium heat. Cook, uncovered, for 20 minutes. Stir often.

Add remaining ingredients. Stir. Continue to cook until thick, stirring often, about 30 minutes more. Pour into hot sterilized jars to within ¼ inch (6 mm) of top. Seal. Makes 2½ pints.

MILLION DOLLAR RELISH

Worth every dollar.

Cucumbers with peel	6 lbs.	3 kg
Onions	2 lbs.	1 kg
Green peppers, seeds removed	3	3
Red peppers, seeds removed	2	2
Coarse (pickling) salt	½ cup	125 mL
Boiling water	10 cups	2.5 L
White vinegar	2½ cups	625 mL
Granulated sugar	5 cups	1.25 L
Mustard seed	2 tbsp.	30 mL
Turmeric	1 tbsp.	15 mL
Cornstarch	2 tbsp.	30 mL
Cold water	2 tbsp.	30 mL

Cut cucumbers, onions, green peppers and red peppers into chunks. Put through food grinder into large pot.

Sprinkle with salt. Pour boiling water over all. Cover and let stand overnight on counter.

In the morning, drain mixture well. Add vinegar, sugar, mustard seed and turmeric. Bring to a boil over medium heat. Stir often. Boil slowly for 30 minutes.

Stir cornstarch into cold water. Stir into boiling pickle until thickened slightly. Pour into hot sterilized jars to within ¼ inch (6 mm) of top. Seal. Makes about 7 pints.

Pictured on page 107.

SWEET PICKLE RELISH

It is easy to make your own. Use in sandwich fillings and hamburgers and hot dogs.

Cucumbers	6 lbs.	2.7 kg
Finely chopped red pepper, packed	¼ cup	60 mL
Coarse (pickling) salt	3⅓ tbsp.	50 mL
Granulated sugar	2⅔ cups	650 mL
Vinegar	1 cup	250 mL
Water	1 cup	250 mL
Mustard seed	1 tsp.	5 mL
Onion powder	½ tsp.	2 mL
Celery salt	½ tsp.	2 mL
Green food coloring (optional)		

Cut cucumbers lengthwise and remove seeds. Small cucumbers are best because of more green peel being added. Put cucumbers and red pepper through food grinder into bowl. Mix in salt. Cover and let stand on counter overnight.

Drain. Turn into large pot. Add remaining ingredients. Bring to a boil on medium heat, stirring until sugar dissolves. Boil for 30 minutes stirring occasionally. If you like, you may add a wee bit of green food coloring to make it a touch greener, like store-bought sweet pickle relish. Pour into hot sterilized jars to within ¼ inch (6 mm) of top. Seal. Makes 4 half pints.

Pictured on page 35.

A fast tricycle is a tot rod.

A mild relish dotted with little red pepper pieces.

Cucumbers with peel	6 lbs.	2.75 kg
Onions	3 lbs.	1.36 kg
Large cauliflower head	1	1
Red peppers, seeded	6	6
Table salt	2 tbsp.	30 mL
DRESSING		
Granulated sugar	3 cups	750 mL
All-purpose flour	½ cup	125 mL
Turmeric	1 tsp.	5 mL
Celery seed	1 tsp.	5 mL
Mustard seed	1 tsp.	5 mL
White vinegar	3 cups	750 mL

Cut up cucumbers, onions, cauliflower and red peppers and run through food grinder. Put in large bowl.

Sprinkle with salt. Cover and let stand overnight on counter. Drain.

Dressing: Stir first 5 ingredients together in large pot.

Mix in vinegar. Cook over medium-high heat, and stir until it boils and thickens. Add ground vegetables. Return to a boil. Cook 10 minutes, stirring occasionally. Pour into hot sterilized jars to within ¼ inch (6 mm) of top. Seal. Makes 8 pints.

Pictured on page 71.

A burned out post office is a terrible case of blackmail.

SPICED PLUMS

An old family recipe. Especially good with baked ham or cold beef. Good served over cream cheese, cottage cheese or just to eat a spoonful.

Prune plums	3½ lbs.	1.6 kg
Granulated sugar	6 cups	1.35 L
Ground cinnamon	1 tbsp.	15 mL
Ground cloves	1½ tsp.	7 mL
Table salt	½ tsp.	2 mL
White vinegar	1½ cups	350 mL

Cut plums in half. Remove stones. If you don't have a food processor, cut each half into at least 8 pieces so skin won't be in large pieces when finished. If you do have a food processor (or blender), cut each half into 3 or 4 pieces. Place in large pot.

Add remaining ingredients. Stir on medium-high until sugar dissolves. Bring to a boil. Boil, stirring occasionally, about 5 minutes until plums are mushy. Cool. Run through food processor in batches. Some bits of skin should show. Return to pot. Bring to a boil once more. Pour into hot sterilized jars to within ¼ inch (6 mm) of top. Seal. Makes 5½ pints.

PANCAKE SYRUP

With this on hand there is no last minute scramble looking for syrup.

Water	3 cups	675 mL
Granulated sugar	3 cups	675 mL
Brown sugar	3 cups	675 mL
Corn syrup	1 cup	225 mL
Lemon juice, fresh or bottled	1 tbsp.	15 mL
Vanilla	1 tbsp.	15 mL
Maple flavoring	1 tbsp.	15 mL

Combine first 4 ingredients in large saucepan. Stir on medium-high until it boils.

Add lemon juice, vanilla and maple flavoring. Stir. Fill hot sterilized bottles to within ¼ inch (6 mm) of top. Seal. Makes 3½ pints.

Pictured on page 89.

SWEET AND SOUR SAUCE

Can or freeze this sauce. This is also good without the soy sauce.

Brown sugar, packed	3 cups	700 mL
All-purpose flour	1/3 cup	75 mL
White vinegar	1½ cups	350 mL
Water	1 cup	250 mL
Soy sauce	¼ cup	60 mL
Paprika	½ tsp.	2 mL

Stir sugar and flour together well in saucepan.

Add vinegar and mix. Add water, soy sauce and paprika. Stir on medium until it boils and thickens. Pour into hot sterilized jars to within ¼ inch (6 mm) from top. Seal. Makes 3½ cups, or 3 half pints and 1 small jar.

WINTER CHILI SAUCE

A good chili sauce to make when you don't have ripe tomatoes, or simply when it is more convenient.

Canned tomatoes (see Note)	28 oz.	796 mL
Large tart apples, finely chopped	3	3
Large onions, finely chopped	2	2
Finely chopped celery	1 cup	250 mL
Red pepper, seeded and finely chopped	1	1
Table salt	1½ tsp.	7 mL
Brown sugar, packed	1 cup	250 mL
Ground cinnamon	½ tsp.	2 mL
Ground cloves	¼ tsp.	1 mL
White vinegar	¾ cup	175 mL

Place first 6 ingredients in saucepan. Bring to a boil over medium heat. Cook, uncovered, about 1¼ hours until tender, stirring occasionally.

Add remaining ingredients. Stir. Return to a boil. Pour into hot sterilized jars to within ¼ inch (6 mm) of top. Seal. Makes 3½ pints.

Note: To use fresh tomatoes, peel and cook 2⅓ pounds (1 kg).

Pictured on page 35.

CHILI SAUCE

If too many tomatoes are ripening too fast, consider this as a solution.

Ripe tomatoes, peeled and diced	12	12
Large onions, finely cut	4	4
Finely chopped celery	1 cup	250 mL
White vinegar	2 cups	500 mL
Brown sugar, packed	2 cups	500 mL
Ground cinnamon	1 tbsp.	15 mL
Ground cloves	1 tsp.	5 mL
Table salt	1 tbsp.	15 mL

Combine all ingredients in large pot. Stir over medium heat until it boils. Simmer, uncovered, for about 1½ hours until thickened, stirring occasionally. Pour into hot sterilized jars to within ¼ inch (6 mm) of top. Seal. Makes 4 pints.

TOMATO SAUCE

A tasty sauce to have on hand. Great for pasta.

Ripe tomatoes, peeled and coarsely chopped	4½ lbs.	1 kg
Medium onions, very finely chopped	3	3
White vinegar	1 cup	250 mL
Garlic cloves, minced	2	2
Bay leaves	4	4
Dried basil	2 tsp.	10 mL
Dried oregano	2 tsp.	10 mL
Table salt	2 tsp.	10 mL
Pepper	½ tsp.	2 mL
Allspice	½ tsp.	2 mL
Granulated sugar	1 cup	250 mL

Combine all ingredients in large pot. Bring to a boil on medium-high, stirring often. Simmer, uncovered, for 1½ to 2 hours, stirring occasionally, until thickened to desired sauce consistency. Add more salt if needed. Pour into hot sterilized jars to ¼ inch (6 mm) from top. Seal. If you would rather, this may be cooled, poured into containers leaving 1 inch (2.5 cm) headroom and frozen. Makes 3½ pints.

MEATY SPAGHETTI SAUCE: Brown 2¼ pounds (1 kg) lean ground beef. Add to Tomato Sauce. Stir. Freeze in 2 cup (500 mL) containers. To can in jars, process in pressure cooker-canner according to instructions.

CRANBERRY SAUCE

Homemade is always the best. Plan to put up plenty.

Cranberries	4 cups	1 L
Water	2 cups	500 mL
Granulated sugar	2 cups	500 mL

Combine cranberries and water in large saucepan. Bring to a boil, covered. Simmer for 20 minutes.

Add sugar. Stir to dissolve. Return to a boil. Boil rapidly for 5 minutes. Pour into hot sterilized jars to within ¼ inch (6 mm) of top. Seal. Will keep in refrigerator at least 4 months after opening. Makes 4 half pints.

CRANBERRY JELLY: Press cooked cranberry-water mixture through food mill or sieve. Add sugar and boil as above.

APRICOT SYRUP

Treat your pancakes. Treat your ice cream, too.

Apricots, halved, pitted and cut up	2 lbs.	1 kg
Water	1 cup	250 mL
Granulated sugar	4 cups	1 L
Lemon juice, fresh and bottled	2 tbsp.	30 mL
Corn syrup	1 tbsp.	15 mL

Purée about ½ apricots and ½ water in blender. Turn into large saucepan. Repeat with second half of apricots and water.

Add sugar, lemon juice and corn syrup. Stir over medium-high heat until sugar dissolves and it comes to a boil. Boil and stir for 5 minutes. Skim. Pour into hot sterilized jars to within ¼ inch (6 mm) of top. Seal. Makes 6 half pints.

Pictured on page 89.

BARBECUE SAUCE

Your tomato patch will help you to make an economical sauce. Freezes well.

Ripe tomatoes	4½ lbs.	2 kg.
Very finely chopped celery	2 cups	500 mL
Very finely chopped green pepper	1½ cups	375 mL
Medium onions, very finely chopped	3	3
Garlic cloves, minced	2	2
Brown sugar, packed	1 cup	250 mL
White vinegar	1 cup	250 mL
Worcestershire sauce	1 tbsp.	15 mL
Paprika	2 tbsp.	30 mL
Mustard powder	1 tbsp.	15 mL
Table salt	2 tsp.	10 mL
Cayenne pepper	¼ tsp.	1 mL
Chili powder	½ tsp.	2 mL
Liquid smoke	½ tsp.	2 mL

Cut tomatoes into chunks and place in large pot. Cook, stirring often, on medium heat until soft. Press through food mill to remove seeds and skin. Return purée to pot.

Add remaining ingredients. Stir well. Bring to a boil on medium heat, stirring often. Simmer for about 1½ hours, stirring occasionally, until thickened. Cool. Smooth in blender. Return purée to pot. Return to a boil. At this point, more paprika may be added for color or less if tomatoes are deep red. Cayenne pepper may be increased for more of a bite. Pour into hot sterilized jars to within ¼ inch (6 mm) of top. Seal. Makes 7 half pints.

Pictured on page 35.

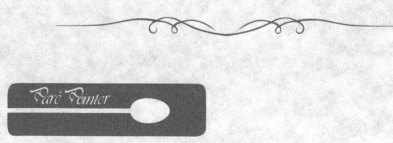

Paré Pointer

An astronaut's watch is better known as a luna-tick.

BLUEBERRY SYRUP

Goes well on plain hotcakes but especially on blueberry hotcakes.

Blueberries	6 cups	1.35 mL
Granulated sugar	1 cup	225 mL
Water	1 cup	225 mL
Corn syrup	⅓ cup	75 mL
Lemon juice, fresh or bottled	2 tsp.	10 mL

Combine all ingredients in large saucepan. Heat and stir on medium-high until it boils. Simmer, covered, for 10 minutes. Strain. Pour into 2 hot sterilized half pints, dividing evenly. Add boiling water if needed to fill within ¼ inch (6 mm) of top. Seal. Makes 2 half pints.

Pictured on page 89.

DRIED TOMATOES

A wonderful appetizer.

Roma tomatoes, halved and seeded	12	12
BRINE		
Cooking oil	1½ cups	300 mL
Thin lemon peel, 1 × ½ inch, (2.5 × 1 cm)	4	4
Black peppercorns	1 tsp.	5 mL
Mustard seeds	½ tsp.	2 mL
Onion salt	½ tsp.	2 mL
Thyme	½ tsp.	2 mL
Basil	½ tsp.	2 mL
Chives	½ tsp.	2 mL
Garlic salt	½ tsp.	2 mL
Rosemary	½ tsp.	2 mL

Lay tomato halves cut side down on racks. Place racks on baking sheets. Dry in 150°F (65°C) oven for about 12 hours. Remove smaller ones as they dry.

Brine: Stir all ingredients together in jar. Add dried tomatoes. Add more cooking oil if necessary to cover. Let stand in refrigerator 1 week before using. Remove with slotted spoon. Makes 24.

SANDWICH SPREAD

Just tart enough.

Green pepper, seeded and finely ground	1	1
Red pepper, seeded and finely ground	1	1
White vinegar	¾ cup	175 mL
Granulated sugar	1 cup	250 mL
Whipping cream	1 cup	250 mL
Butter or margarine	½ cup	125 mL
Coarse (pickling) salt	2 tsp.	10 mL
Dry mustard powder	1 tbsp.	15 mL
Large eggs	3	3
All-purpose flour	¼ cup	60 mL
Grated medium Cheddar cheese	1 cup	250 mL

Combine first 8 ingredients in heavy saucepan. Heat on medium-high, stirring often as it comes to a boil.

In small bowl, mix eggs and flour until smooth. Stir into boiling mixture until it returns to a boil and thickens.

Stir in cheese until it melts. Pour into hot sterilized jars to within ¼ inch (6 mm) of top or cool 15 minutes, fill containers to within 1 inch (2.5 cm) of top, cover and freeze. Seal. Makes 4 to 5 half pints.

Pictured on page 71.

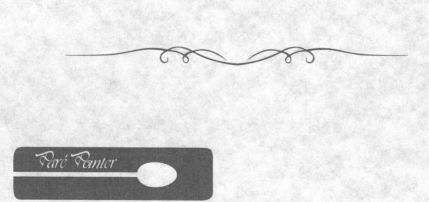

Paré Pointer

This is how to start a flea race "One, two, flea, go!"

FREEZER TOMATOES

Use garden vine-ripened tomatoes to enjoy in the months ahead.

Ripe tomatoes, to make 4 cups (900 mL) cut up	**2 lbs.**	**900 g**
Tomato juice	**½ cup**	**125 mL**
Granulated sugar	**2 tsp.**	**10 mL**
Table salt	**1 tsp.**	**5 mL**

To peel tomatoes, put into boiling water for about 30 seconds, then peel. Measure 4 cups (900 mL). Put all ingredients together into saucepan. Bring to a boil. Simmer for 10 minutes, stirring 2 or 3 times. Cool. Pack into containers, leaving 1 inch (2.5 cm) room for expansion. Freeze. Makes 4 cups (900 mL).

KETCHUP

Makes enough for one bottle to use right away, or make several recipes to preserve. Economical.

Tomato paste,	**5½ oz.**	**56 mL**
White vinegar	**½ cup**	**125 mL**
Granulated sugar	**¼ cup**	**60 mL**
Onion powder	**¾ tsp.**	**4 mL**
Table salt	**¾ tsp.**	**4 mL**
Ground cloves	**⅛ tsp.**	**0.5 mL**

Stir all ingredients together well in saucepan. Stir on medium heat until it comes to a boil. Pour into hot sterilized jar to within ¼ inch (6 mm) of top. Seal if planning to store on the shelf, or refrigerate for immediate use. Keeps for at least 8 months in refrigerator. Makes 1 half pint.

Pictured on page 35.

Paré Pointer

The ruler of a country can be the Czar, his wife the Czarina and their children Czardines.

SNAP BEANS

So called because they are a snap to make.

Green string beans, cut in 1 inch (2.5 cm) lengths	16 cups	3.6 L
Water	32 cups	7.2 L
Coarse (pickling) salt	¾ cup	175 mL
White vinegar	½ cup	125 mL

Pack beans loosely in jars, leaving 1 inch (2.5 cm) headroom.

Measure water, salt and vinegar into large saucepan. Bring to a boil. Pour over beans up to ½ inch (12 mm) from top. Secure lids. Process in hot water bath for 30 minutes. This is very good heated in liquid from jar, or heat in fresh water if desired. Makes 8 pints or 4 quarts.

Pictured on page 125.

CRANBERRY KETCHUP

Surprise your chicken with this.

Cranberries, fresh or frozen	1¼ lbs.	570 g
Water to cover		
Cranberry pulp	1½ cups	350 mL
White vinegar	½ cup	125 mL
Granulated sugar	2 cups	450 mL
Ground cinnamon	1 tsp.	5 mL
Pepper	¾ tsp.	4 mL
Ground cloves	½ tsp.	2 mL
Table salt	½ tsp.	2 mL

Cook cranberries in water until skins pop. Drain. Turn cranberries into food processor. Process until broken down into pulp.

Combine pulp, vinegar, sugar and 4 spices in large saucepan. Simmer, uncovered, about 20 minutes, stirring often, until thick. Pour into hot sterilized jars to within ¼ inch (6 mm) of top. Seal. Makes 2 half pints and 1 small jar.

RHUBARB KETCHUP

Use this tangy spread on meat or sandwiches. Good flavor.

Diced rhubarb	6 cups	1.35 L
Chopped onion	4 cups	900 mL
Diced celery	1½ cups	375 mL
Canned tomatoes, drained and mashed (see Note)	28 oz.	796 mL
Granulated sugar	3 cups	700 mL
White vinegar	2 cups	450 mL
Ground cinnamon	2 tsp.	10 mL
Ground cloves	1 tsp.	5 mL
Table salt	1 tsp.	5 mL
Pepper	1 tsp.	5 mL
Mixed pickling spices, tied in double layer of cheesecloth	1 tsp.	5 mL

Measure all ingredients into large saucepan. Bring to a boil over medium heat. Simmer, uncovered, about 35 minutes, stirring often, until vegetables are cooked and mixture is thickened. Discard spice bag. May be left as is or put through food mill or sieve to make smooth and remove seeds. Reheat to boiling. Pour into hot sterilized jars to within ¼ inch (6 mm) of top. Seal. Makes 3½ pints.

Note: Peeled, cubed and cooked tomatoes may be used, about 2⅓ pounds (1 kg).

CANNED TOMATOES

A good use for your tomato patch.

Tomatoes, peeled	5½ lbs.	2.5 kg
Bottled lemon juice (not fresh), per pint	1 tbsp.	15 mL
Coarse (pickling) salt, per pint	½ tsp.	2 mL
Granulated sugar, per pint	½ tsp.	2 mL

Tomatoes may be left whole or cut up. Place in large pot. Heat on medium until starting to boil. Pour into hot sterilized jars to within ½ inch (12 mm) of top.

Add lemon juice, salt and sugar to each pint. Secure lids. Process in hot water bath 35 minutes for pints, 45 minutes for quarts. Makes 4 pints.

SAUERKRAUT

Homemade is the best. Start with a small quantity. Increase as desired.

Cabbage, shredded	**6 lbs.**	**2.72 kg**
Coarse (pickling) salt	**4 tbsp.**	**60 mL**

Place ¼ of shredded cabbage and 1 tbsp. (15 mL) salt in small crock. Tamp it down to bruise cabbage and start juice formation. A baseball bat is ideal for tamping large amounts and a potato masher for small amounts. Repeat until all cabbage and salt are used. Cover with inverted plate or round board. Weigh it down with a rock or something heavy enough so the brine comes up to the cover but not over it. Cover with plastic wrap. Leave to ferment at room temperature. It will also ferment at a cooler temperature but will take a little longer. Check daily and skim off froth that rises. Make sure cabbage is immersed. As soon as fermentation is complete, there will be no more bubbles rising to the top and the juice will have disappeared back into the cabbage. This will take about 10 to 12 days.

Pack into hot sterilized jars to within ½ inch (12 mm) of top, with enough brine to cover. If more brine is needed, dissolve 2 tbsp. (30 mL) coarse (pickling) salt in 2 cups (500 mL) water. Wipe tops of jars clean. Secure lids. Process in hot water bath 35 minutes for pints, 40 minutes for quarts. Makes 3 quarts.

Butter's Table Courtesy Of:
Ethan Allen Home Interiors

China Courtesy Of:
Reed's China And Gift Shop

Ice Cream Dish Courtesy Of:
The Bay China Dept.

GOLDEN MUSTARD

Fairly mild. Not too sweet. A good recipe for beginners.

All-purpose flour	²/₃ cup	150 mL
Granulated sugar	³/₄ cup	175 mL
Dry mustard powder	1½ tsp.	7 mL
Table salt	2 tsp.	10 mL
Turmeric	1 tsp.	5 mL
Water	³/₄ cup	175 mL
White vinegar	1 cup	225 mL
Water	²/₃ cup	150 mL
Margarine	3 tbsp.	50 mL
Lemon juice, fresh or bottled	2 tsp.	10 mL

Stir first 5 ingredients together well in saucepan.

Mix in first amount of water until smooth.

Add remaining ingredients. Stir over medium heat until it boils and thickens. Pour into hot sterilized jars to within ¼ inch (6 mm) of top. Seal. Makes 2 half pints with ²/₃ cup (150 mL) left over to use right away.

Pictured on page 35.

HONEY MUSTARD DRESSING

A snap to make. Be prepared to share the recipe. Wonderful with salads.

Olive oil (or cooking oil)	1 cup	225 mL
Tarragon vinegar	¼ cup	60 mL
Creamed honey (not liquid)	⅓ cup	75 mL
Dijon mustard	⅓ cup	75 mL
Lemon juice, fresh or bottled	2 tbsp.	30 mL
Garlic clove	1	1

Place all ingredients in blender. Blend until smooth. Put into container. Cover. Stores in refrigerator for at least 6 months. If too thick as it stands, run through blender before using. Makes generous 1 pint.

HERB VINEGAR

Use in a marinade for meat. Also good with salads.

Sprig of basil, 5 inch (13 mm) length	1	1
Sprig of oregano, 5 inch (13 mm) length	1	1
White vinegar	**2 cups**	**450 mL**

Place basil and oregano in pint sealer or tall slim bottle. Fill with vinegar. Cover tightly. Let stand 4 weeks in a cool place. Herb sprigs can be removed or left in as your taste indicates. Keeps at least 1 year. Makes 1 pint.

RASPBERRY VINEGAR

Delicate flavor, delicate color. Especially good with a combined greens and fruit salad.

Mashed raspberries	**½ cup**	**125 mL**
White vinegar, to fill		

Place raspberries in pint jar. Add vinegar to fill jar. Cover. Let stand on counter for 1 week. Strain. Pour into fancy bottle. Raspberries may be left in vinegar for several weeks for more strength if desired. Keeps at least 1 year. Makes about 1 half pint.

Pictured on page 17.

RASPBERRY DRESSING: Stir in granulated sugar or liquid sweetener to taste to make a wonderful dressing for a tossed salad.

Paré Pointer

The policeman was on his way to arrest the ghost for not having a haunting license.

BASIL VINEGAR

For gift giving, place a fresh basil sprig in fancy bottle of strained vinegar. Use on tomato and pasta salad.

Sprigs of basil	2-3	2-3
White vinegar	2 cups	500 mL

Place basil in jar. Add vinegar. Cover. Let stand in cool place for 4 weeks. Taste to see if flavorful enough. If it is, strain before using. If it isn't strong enough, let stand a few more days. Basil twig may be left in bottle for looks. Keeps at least 1 year. Makes about 1 pint.

Pictured on page 17.

CHIVE VINEGAR

A mild hint of chive flavor. Use as any vinegar.

Chives, length of jar height or 1 inch (2.5 cm) lengths		
Lemon peel, 1 inch (2.5 cm) square	1	1
Black peppercorns	4	4
Mustard seeds	3	3
White vinegar, to fill		

Fill pint jar loosely with chives. Add lemon peel, peppercorns and mustard seed. Fill with vinegar. Cover. Let stand in cool place for 4 weeks. Strain into pretty bottle. Two or three lengths of chives can be left in bottle for looks. Keeps at least 1 year. Makes about 1 pint.

Pictured on page 17.

BLUEBERRY VINEGAR

A colored vinegar. Use for salads.

Blueberries	¾ cup	175 mL
White vinegar, to fill		

Crush blueberries and put into pint jar. Fill jar with white vinegar. Cover and let stand in cool place for 3 days, stirring each day. Strain and fill bottle or leave in for stronger flavor. Keeps at least 1 year. Makes about 1 half pint.

DILL VINEGAR

Try this with fish.

Heads of dill	2	2
White vinegar	¾ cup	175 mL
Cider vinegar	¼ cup	60 mL

Place heads of dill in pint jar. Fill with vinegars. Cover. Let stand in dark cool place for 3 weeks. May be strained or leave dill in longer for a bit stronger flavor. Leave a small portion of head of dill for looks. Keeps at least 1 year. Makes 1 half pint.

Pictured on page 17.

GARLIC VINEGAR

Easy to make. This has a lengthy standing time.

Garlic cloves, halved	6	6
Lemon juice, fresh or bottled	2 tsp.	10 mL
Black peppercorns	10	10
White vinegar or cider vinegar	2 cups	500 mL

Place garlic, lemon juice and peppercorns in pint jar or tall slim bottle. Fill with vinegar. Cover tightly. Let stand for 6 weeks in a cool place before using. When strong enough to your liking, strain. Keeps at least 1 year. Makes 1 pint.

GARLIC OIL

Fry your own croutons in this.

Garlic cloves, peeled	2	2
Canola oil (or olive oil)	½ cup	125 mL

Cut garlic cloves in quarters and combine with canola oil in jar. Cover. Let stand 3 or 4 days in refrigerator. Remove garlic. Use with salads and for brushing barbecuing meat. Keeps for up to 2 weeks only. Must be refrigerated. Makes ½ cup (125 mL).

Pictured on page 17.

DILLED OIL: Omit garlic cloves. Add 1 head of dill.

TARRAGON VINEGAR

Especially good for fish and chicken.

Sprigs of tarragon, about 5 inches (13 cm) each	4	4
Garlic clove, peeled	1	1
Lemon peel, 1 inch (2.5 cm) square	2	2
Black peppercorns	5	5
White vinegar, to fill		

Fill pint jar carefully with tarragon without bruising. Add garlic clove and lemon peel and peppercorns. Fill jar with vinegar. Cover. Let stand in cool place for 4 weeks. Strain. Return 1 sprig of tarragon to bottle for looks. Keeps at least 1 year. Makes a scant 1 pint.

TARRAGON RED WINE VINEGAR: Use red wine vinegar instead of white vinegar for a great variation.

Pictured on page 17.

BARBECUE OIL

Brush this on steaks, fish, seafood or any meat before grilling. Try also in salads. Fry croutons in this.

Garlic cloves, peeled	2	2
Bay leaves	2	2
Black peppercorns	6	6
Mustard seed	4	4
Onion slivers	2	2
Canola oil (or olive oil)	1/2 **cup**	**125 mL**

Place first 5 ingredients in any jar that holds 1/2 cup (125 mL).

Pour canola oil over top. Cover. Let stand in refrigerator for at least 4 days before using. Keeps up to 2 weeks only. Must be refrigerated. Makes 1 half pint.

HERBED OIL

Use on grilled meat, seafood or salad. Great for frying croutons.

Sprig of rosemary, about 4 inches (10 cm) long	1	1
Sprig of basil	1	1
Sprig of thyme		
Lemon peel, 2 × ½ inch (5 × 12 mm)	1	1
Orange peel, 2 × ½ inch (5 × 12 mm)	1	1
Red pepper, tiny whole hot one or 2-3 strips bell pepper		
Whole cloves	2	2
Mustard seed	6	6
Black peppercorns	2	2
Canola oil (or olive oil)	1 cup	250 mL

Place first 9 ingredients in tall narrow bottle that holds 1 cup (250 mL).

Add canola oil using more or less as needed to come to top of bottle. Cover. Let stand at least 1 week in cool, dark place or in refrigerator before using. Makes 1 half pint.

WINTER VINEGAR

Flavor your salad dressing with this.

Celery seed	2 tbsp.	30 mL
Parsley flakes	⅓ cup	75 mL
Black peppercorns	1 tsp.	5 mL
Granulated sugar	1 tbsp.	15 mL
Onion powder	½ tsp.	2 mL
Garlic powder	¼ tsp.	1 mL
Mustard seed	¼ tsp.	1 mL
Whole cloves	3	3
Bay leaf	1	1
White vinegar	3 cups	700 mL

Measure first 9 ingredients into quart bottle.

Add vinegar. Cover. Let stand 2 weeks in cool place. Strain through double layer of cheesecloth before using. To use same day, bring mixture to a boil. Remove from heat. Let stand 2 hours. Strain. Keeps at least 1 year. Makes 1½ pints.

Pictured on page 17.

Throughout this book measurements are given in Conventional and Metric measure. To compensate for differences between the two measurements due to rounding, a full metric measure is not always used. The cup used is the standard 8 fluid ounce. Temperature is given in degrees Fahrenheit and Celsius. Baking pan measurements are in inches and centimetres as well as quarts and litres. An exact metric conversion is given below as well as the working equivalent (Standard Measure).

OVEN TEMPERATURES

Fahrenheit (°F)	Celsius (°C)
175°	80°
200°	95°
225°	110°
250°	120°
275°	140°
300°	150°
325°	160°
350°	175°
375°	190°
400°	205°
425°	220°
450°	230°
475°	240°
500°	260°

SPOONS

Conventional Measure	Metric Exact Conversion Millilitre (mL)	Metric Standard Measure Millilitre (mL)
1/4 teaspoon (tsp.)	1.2 mL	1 mL
1/2 teaspoon (tsp.)	2.4 mL	2 mL
1 teaspoon (tsp.)	4.7 mL	5 mL
2 teaspoons (tsp.)	9.4 mL	10 mL
1 tablespoon (tbsp.)	14.2 mL	15 mL

CUPS

	Metric Exact Conversion	Metric Standard Measure
1/4 cup (4 tbsp.)	56.8 mL	50 mL
1/3 cup (5 1/3 tbsp.)	75.6 mL	75 mL
1/2 cup (8 tbsp.)	113.7 mL	125 mL
2/3 cup (10 2/3 tbsp.)	151.2 mL	150 mL
3/4 cup (12 tbsp.)	170.5 mL	175 mL
1 cup (16 tbsp.)	227.3 mL	250 mL
4 1/2 cups	1022.9 mL	1000 mL (1 L)

DRY MEASUREMENTS

Ounces (oz.)	Grams (g)	Grams (g)
1 oz.	28.3 g	30 g
2 oz.	56.7 g	55 g
3 oz.	85.0 g	85 g
4 oz.	113.4 g	125 g
5 oz.	141.7 g	140 g
6 oz.	170.1 g	170 g
7 oz.	198.4 g	200 g
8 oz.	226.8 g	250 g
16 oz.	453.6 g	500 g
32 oz.	907.2 g	1000 g (1 kg)

PANS, CASSEROLES

Conventional Inches	Metric Centimetres	Conventional Quart (qt.)	Metric Litre (L)
8x8 inch	20x20 cm	1 2/3 qt.	2 L
9x9 inch	22x22 cm	2 qt.	2.5 L
9x13 inch	22x33 cm	3 1/3 qt.	4 L
10x15 inch	25x38 cm	1 qt.	1.2 L
11x17 inch	28x43 cm	1 1/4 qt.	1.5 L
8x2 inch round	20x5 cm	1 2/3 qt.	2 L
9x2 inch round	22x5 cm	2 qt.	2.5 L
10x4 1/2 inch tube	25x11 cm	4 1/4 qt.	5 L
8x4x3 inch loaf	20x10x7 cm	1 1/4 qt.	1.5 L
9x5x3 inch loaf	23x12x7 cm	1 2/3 qt.	2 L

INDEX

If you don't see Company's Coming where you shop, ask your retailer to give us a call. Meanwhile, we offer a mail order service for your convenience.

Just indicate the books you would like below. Then complete the reverse page and send your order with payment to us.

Buying a gift? Enclose a personal note or card and we will be pleased to send it with your order.

Deduct $5.00 for every $35.00 ordered.

See reverse.

SAVE $5.00!

Company's Coming COOKBOOKS

Company's Coming Publishing Limited
Box 8037, Station F
Edmonton, Alberta, Canada T6H 4N9
Tel: (403) 450-6223

MAIL ORDER COUPON

QUANTITY • HARD COVER BOOK •

Jean Paré's Favorites - Volume One

	TOTAL BOOKS	TOTAL PRICE

TOTAL $17.95 + $1.50 shipping = **$19.45 each** x _____ = $ _____

ENGLISH

QUANTITY • SOFT COVER BOOKS •

150 Delicious Squares	Pasta
Casseroles	Cakes
Muffins & More	Barbecues
Salads	Dinners of the World
Appetizers	Lunches
Desserts	Pies
Soups & Sandwiches	Light Recipes
Holiday Entertaining	Microwave Cooking
Cookies	Preserves
Vegetables	Light Casseroles (Sept. '94)
Main Courses	

TOTAL BOOKS   TOTAL PRICE

TOTAL $10.95 + $1.50 shipping = **$12.45 each** x _____ = $ _____

QUANTITY • PINT SIZE BOOKS •

Finger Food
Party Planning
Buffets

TOTAL BOOKS   TOTAL PRICE

TOTAL $4.99 + $1.00 shipping = **$5.99 each** x _____ = $ _____

FRENCH

QUANTITY • SOFT COVER BOOKS •

150 délicieux carrés	Recettes légères
Les casseroles	Les salades
Muffins et plus	La cuisson au micro-ondes
Les dîners	Les pâtes
Les barbecues	Les conserves
Les tartes	Les casseroles légères (sept. '94)
Délices des fêtes	

TOTAL BOOKS   TOTAL PRICE

TOTAL $10.95 + $1.50 shipping = **$12.45 each** x _____ = $ _____

Please fill in reverse side of this coupon   **TOTAL PRICE FOR ALL BOOKS**
(See reverse) * $ _____

SAVE $5.00!

Deduct $5.00 for every $35.00 ordered.

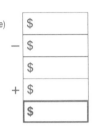

COOKBOOKS®

Company's Coming Publishing Limited
Box 8037, Station F
Edmonton, Alberta, Canada T6H 4N9
Tel: (403) 450-6223

MAIL ORDER COUPON

TOTAL PRICE FOR ALL BOOKS (from reverse)		$
Less $5.00 for every $35.00 ordered	—	$
SUBTOTAL		$
Canadian residents add G.S.T.	+	$
TOTAL AMOUNT ENCLOSED		$

Gift Giving

• Let us help you with your gift giving!

• We will send cookbooks directly to the recipients of your choice if you give us their names and addresses.

• Be sure to specify the titles of the cookbooks you wish to send to each person.

• If you would like to enclose your personal note or card, we will be pleased to include it with your gift order.

GIFT SHIPPING ADDRESS

Send my gift of Company's Coming Cookbooks listed on the reverse side of this coupon, to:

Name:

Street:

City: Province/State:

Postal Code/Zip: Tel: (   )   —

Company's Coming Cookbooks make excellent gifts. Birthdays, bridal showers, Mother's Day, Father's Day, graduation or any occasion... collect them all! Remember to enclose your personal note or card and we will be pleased to send it with your order.

If you don't see Company's Coming where you shop, ask your retailer to give us a call. Meanwhile, we offer a mail order service for your convenience.

Just indicate the books you would like below. Then complete the reverse page and send your order with payment to us.

Buying a gift? Enclose a personal note or card and we will be pleased to send it with your order.

Deduct $5.00 for every $35.00 ordered.

See reverse.

SAVE $5.00!

Company's Coming Publishing Limited
Box 8037, Station F
Edmonton, Alberta, Canada T6H 4N9
Tel: (403) 450-6223

MAIL ORDER COUPON

QUANTITY • HARD COVER BOOK •

		TOTAL BOOKS	TOTAL PRICE
	Jean Paré's Favorites - Volume One		

TOTAL $17.95 + $1.50 shipping = **$19.45 each** x ___ = $ ___

ENGLISH

QUANTITY • SOFT COVER BOOKS •

150 Delicious Squares	Pasta
Casseroles	Cakes
Muffins & More	Barbecues
Salads	Dinners of the World
Appetizers	Lunches
Desserts	Pies
Soups & Sandwiches	Light Recipes
Holiday Entertaining	Microwave Cooking
Cookies	Preserves
Vegetables	Light Casseroles *(Sept '94)*
Main Courses	

TOTAL BOOKS   TOTAL PRICE

TOTAL $10.95 + $1.50 shipping = **$12.45 each** x ___ = $ ___

QUANTITY • PINT SIZE BOOKS •

Finger Food	
Party Planning	
Buffets	

TOTAL BOOKS   TOTAL PRICE

TOTAL $4.99 + $1.00 shipping = **$5.99 each** x ___ = $ ___

FRENCH

QUANTITY • SOFT COVER BOOKS •

150 délicieux carrés	Recettes légères
Les casseroles	Les salades
Muffins et plus	La cuisson au micro-ondes
Les dîners	Les pâtes
Les barbecues	Les conserves
Les tartes	Les casseroles légères *(sept '94)*
Délices des fêtes	

TOTAL BOOKS   TOTAL PRICE

TOTAL $10.95 + $1.50 shipping = **$12.45 each** x ___ = $ ___

***Please fill in reverse side of this coupon ***

TOTAL PRICE FOR ALL BOOKS
(See reverse) *

$ ___

Deduct $5.00 for every $35.00 ordered.

COOKBOOKS

Company's Coming Publishing Limited
Box 8037, Station F
Edmonton, Alberta, Canada T6H 4N9
Tel: (403) 450-6223

MAIL ORDER COUPON

TOTAL PRICE FOR ALL BOOKS (from reverse)	$
Less $5.00 for every $35.00 ordered −	$
SUBTOTAL	$
Canadian residents add G.S.T. +	$
TOTAL AMOUNT ENCLOSED	$

- **ORDERS OUTSIDE CANADA:** *Must be paid in U.S. funds by cheque or money order drawn on Canadian or U.S. bank.*

- *Prices subject to change without prior notice.*

- *Sorry, no C.O.D.'s*

- **MAKE CHEQUE OR MONEY ORDER PAYABLE TO:** *COMPANY'S COMING PUBLISHING LIMITED*

Gift Giving
We Make It Easy...You Make It Delicious

Let us help you with your gift giving! We will send cookbooks directly to the recipients of your choice if you give us their names and addresses. Be sure to specify the titles of the cookbooks you wish to send to each person.

Send the Company's Coming Cookbooks listed on the reverse side of this coupon to:

Name:

Street:

City: Province/State:

Postal Code/Zip: Tel: (   )   —

Company's Coming Cookbooks make excellent gifts. Birthdays, bridal showers, Mother's Day, Father's Day, graduation or any occasion... collect them all! Remember to enclose your personal note or card and we will be pleased to send it with your order.